PENGUIN CLASSICS

DOVEGLION: COLLECTED POEMS

JOSÉ GARCIA VILLA (1908–1997): Poet, critic, short story writer, and painter José Garcia Villa was born in Singalong, Manila, on August 5, 1908. Villa attended the University of the Philippines in 1929. He first studied medicine and then changed to law, but he was always interested in writing, and as a law student he wrote short stories and poetry. Villa moved to the United States in 1930. He studied at the University of New Mexico where he founded a literary magazine, *Clay*, and later did postgraduate work at Columbia University. He worked as an associate editor at New Directions Publishing in New York from 1949 to 1951 and was director of the poetry workshop at City College of the City University of New York from 1952 to 1960; from 1964 to 1973 he taught poetry workshops at the New School for Social Research in New York City. Villa also served as cultural attaché to the Philippine mission to the United Nations from 1952 to 1963, and beginning in 1968 he was adviser on cultural affairs to the president of the Philippines. His first U.S. collection of poetry, *Have Come, Am Here* (1942) was published by Viking and received critical acclaim. *Volume Two* (1949), another collection of poetry, was awarded the Bollingen Prize that year. Two other collections of Villa's poetry are *Selected Poems and New* (1958) and *Appassionata: Poems in Praise of Love* (1979). Villa received the American Academy of Arts and Letters' Poetry Award, the Shelley Memorial Award, and the Guggenheim, Bollingen, and Rockefeller fellowships for poetry. In 1973 he was named National Artist for Literature in the Philippines. He died on February 7, 1997, in New York.

JOHN EDWIN COWEN is professor of Education/Literacy at Fairleigh Dickinson University. He earned his doctorate at Columbia University. Dr. Cowen is the author and editor of seven books, most recently: *Literacy for Children in an Information Age* (Thomson-Wadsworth) and *Parlement of Giraffes: Poems for Children Eight to Eighty by José Garcia Villa* (Anvil). Cowen studied poetry with José Garcia Villa from 1964 to 1997 and serves as Mr. Villa's literary trustee. He is copublisher of Villa's

Appassionata: Poems in Praise of Love (King and Cowen) and *Bravo: The Poet's Magazine* (Bravo Editions). Cowen has published numerous essays and articles on Villa, most recently in the *Philippines Free Press* and, notably, in *Spring: The Journal of the E. E. Cummings Society* 10, "Doveglion: The E. E. Cummings/José Garcia Villa Connection." Cowen is also a first prize–winning poet in *Parnassus Literary Journal*'s International Competition. His book of poems, *Mathematics of Love*, will be published in 2008.

LUIS H. FRANCIA is an award-winning poet, writer, and teacher at the Asian/Pacific/American Studies Program at New York University. Francia is the author of the poetry collection *Museum of Absences* (2004). His semiautobiographical critique of the Philippines, *Eye of the Fish: A Personal Archipelago*, won both the 2002 PEN Center Open Book Award and the 2002 Asian American Literary Award. Other books include *The Arctic Archipelago and Other Poems* (1992) and *Memories of Overdevelopment: Reviews and Essays of Two Decades* (1998). He is the editor of *Brown River, White Ocean: An Anthology of Twentieth-Century Philippine Literature in English* (1993) and coeditor of *Flippin': Filipinos on America* (1996) and *Vestiges of War: The Philippine-American War and the Aftermath of an Imperial Dream, 1899–1999* (2002). He serves as cochair of the board of trustees of the Asian American Writers' Workshop and has written for the *Village Voice*, the *Daily News*, and the *Nation*. He is a columnist for the *Inquirer* in Manila.

JOSÉ GARCIA VILLA

Doveglion: Collected Poems

Introduction by
LUIS H. FRANCIA

Edited by
JOHN EDWIN COWEN

PENGUIN BOOKS

PENGUIN BOOKS
Published by the Penguin Group
Penguin Group (USA) Inc., 375 Hudson Street, New York, New York 10014, U.S.A.
Penguin Group (Canada), 90 Eglinton Avenue East, Suite 700, Toronto,
Ontario, Canada M4P 2Y3 (a division of Pearson Penguin Canada Inc.)
Penguin Books Ltd, 80 Strand, London WC2R 0RL, England
Penguin Ireland, 25 St Stephen's Green, Dublin 2, Ireland (a division of Penguin Books Ltd)
Penguin Group (Australia), 250 Camberwell Road, Camberwell,
Victoria 3124, Australia (a division of Pearson Australia Group Pty Ltd)
Penguin Books India Pvt Ltd, 11 Community Centre, Panchsheel Park, New Delhi – 110 017, India
Penguin Group (NZ), 67 Apollo Drive, Rosedale, North Shore 0632,
New Zealand (a division of Pearson New Zealand Ltd)
Penguin Books (South Africa) (Pty) Ltd, 24 Sturdee Avenue, Rosebank, Johannesburg 2196, South Africa

Penguin Books Ltd, Registered Offices: 80 Strand, London WC2R 0RL, England

First published in Penguin Books 2008

LIBRARY OF CONGRESS CATALOGING IN PUBLICATION DATA
Villa, José Garcia.
Doveglion : collection poems / José Garcia Villa ; edited by John Edwin Cowen ; introduction by Luis H.
Francia.
    p.   cm.—(Penguin classics)
Includes bibliographical references.
ISBN 978-0-14-310535-0
1. Cowen, John E.   II. Title.
PR9550.9.V48D68   2008
821'.912—dc22   2008028404

Set in Sabon

146028962

DOVEGLION

he isn't looking at anything
he isn't looking for something
he isn't looking
he is seeing

what

not something outside himself
not anything inside himself
but himself

himself how

not as some anyone
not as any someone

only as a noone(who is everyone)

E. E. Cummings

E. E. Cummings's poem, "Doveglion"—written in praise of José Garcia Villa—first appeared opposite his wife, Marion Morehouse's photograph in their 1962 collaborative book *Adventures in Value* (New York: Harcourt, Brace, 1962).

Contents

DOVEGLION: COLLECTED POEMS

HAVE COME, AM HERE
(The Viking Press, 1942)

LYRICS: I

LYRICS: II

LYRICS: III

LYRICS: IV

DIVINE POEMS

from *VOLUME TWO*
(New Directions, 1949)

These poems from Volume Two *were selected, rewritten and/or rever-
sified by José Garcia Villa and are reprinted here as they appeared in*
Selected Poems and New.

APHORISMS, I

CAPRICES

EARLY POEMS

LYRICS

PHILOSOPHICA

from *APPASSIONATA: POEMS IN PRAISE OF LOVE*
(King and Cowen, 1979)

DUO-TECHNIQUE AND XOCERISMS

DUO-TECHNIQUE POEMS AND ADAPTATIONS

XOCERISMS

The Gotham Book Mart reception (November 9, 1948) for Dame Edith and Osbert Sitwell (seated, center) gathers together some of the most important poets, authors, and critics of the 1940s. Standing to the right of Dame Edith Sitwell is Asian American poet José Garcia Villa—whom Sitwell championed as one of the world's greatest contemporary poets in her prominent 1954 London Times Literary Supplement *article, which also featured Villa's poem, "The Anchored Angel." Clockwise around Villa are W. H. Auden (seated on ladder), Elizabeth Bishop, Marianne Moore, Randall Jarrell, Delmore Schwartz, Charles Henri Ford, William Rose Benet, Stephen Spender, Marya Zaturenska, Horace Gregory, Tennessee Williams, Richard Eberhart, and Gore Vidal.*

Introduction

I knew of him, of course. In Manila, he possessed an outsized reputation both for his bohemian ways and, more importantly, his pronouncements on the state of Philippine letters. His selections of stories and poems that he judged worthy of notice had all the weight of papal encyclicals. When Filipino writers referred to José Garcia Villa as the "pope of Greenwich Village," they were only half joking. And here I was, one spring evening in the early 1970s, at Smith's Bar, a nondescript watering hole in the Village. Once a week, he and his poetry-workshop students from the nearby New School for Social Research would walk over to Smith's for drinks (a very dry martini in José's case) and animated, all-night conversations.

New to the city and to the wide precincts of America, I was living with Henry, my oldest brother, now deceased, and his lovely wife, Beatriz. It was they who had brought me to meet José. Nothing remarkable marked that night. Needless to say, I was disappointed. Like any other impressionable young writer meeting a legendary figure, I expected the poet to display verbal pyrotechnics. After all, he was notorious for his withering put-downs, which made me understandably wary, for much as I wished to hear his mots justes—and I did quite often later on—my desire lacked any trace of masochism. He was unfailingly polite that night, no doubt owing to the presence of my brother who, being a filmmaker, had no need for José's imprimatur and could therefore banter with him. And he was very fond of Beatriz, herself a writer but not a poet.

I don't remember what I said, or replied, to the questions José put to me—the same sort of questions any fellow expatriate would have asked, out of politeness and friendly curiosity. The following year, I enrolled in his New School course, and having completed that (or "graduated," a favorite Villa term), I then signed up for the workshop at his apartment in the West Village, and studied with him for close to two more years. To survive and even flourish in José's workshop, you had to have a strong ego or cultivate one. Little time was spent on niceties. Works that deserved to be killed got killed unceremoniously; words were often exchanged, and not only with fellow students. One got a tangible sense of what worked and what didn't—above all else, José made clear what rendered lines poetry rather than just chopped-up prose. I didn't always agree with his critiques, but they were well thought out, even provocative. Moreover, I was a novice; and he, the master. He could be a goad, but mostly he was a catalyst. He had, in sum, a whole lot of *there* there.

José's apartment was a different story. Unlike the elegance and sensual spareness of his poetry, the flat on Greenwich Street revealed a pack rat. Books, papers, magazines, bric-a-brac of uncommon variety, claimed ever-dwindling space. At one end was a bust of Saint Thérèse, "the Little Flower" of Lisieux. At another was a self-portrait by E. E. Cummings, lending the workshop proceedings a magisterial grace. By the time I studied with him, José had for the most part stopped writing poetry—a fact that didn't bother me. What he had accomplished and, more importantly, his critical powers were what mattered. Like Laura Riding, whom he greatly admired and who had ceased to write poems shortly after her *Collected Poems* came out in 1938, he realized that he had reached his poetic limit around the time his *Selected Poems and New* was published in 1958. Not wishing to fall into the trap of repeating himself, as, he kept reminding us, he saw other poets doing, he devoted himself to creating a philosophy of poetry and imparting his insights through the workshop. As suddenly as he had burst onto the literary scene, he retreated into relative obscurity, renouncing, as it were, the pomp of the papacy for the ascetic joys of monkhood—except for his daily martini.

Even before he electrified the New York poetry world, Villa had, as an enfant terrible, already blazed a trail through the literary landscape of Manila, scandalizing its bourgeoisie with a series of poems titled Man Songs. It's easy to see how, for instance, "The Coconut Poem" (written when the poet was seventeen years old) shocked a conservative, heavily Roman Catholic society with its sexual imagery:

> The coconuts have ripened,
> They are like nipples to the tree.
> > (A woman has only two nipples,
> > There are many women-lives in a coconut tree.)
> Soon the coconuts will grow heavy and full:
> I shall pick one . . . many . . .
> > Like a child I shall suck their milk,
> > I shall suck out of coconuts little white songs:
> > I shall be reminded of many women.
> . . . .
> I shall kiss a coconut because it is the nipple of a woman. [239][1]

Considered too erotic, such poems got the novice writer tried and fined by the courts for obscenity and suspended from the state-run University of the Philippines—founded, coincidentally, in 1908, the year of his birth. At the time he was also writing fiction, well enough to win first-prize money in a short story competition, which he used for passage to the United States. In 1930, he enrolled at the University of New Mexico to study medicine and promptly started a literary magazine, Clay. Among the writers he published were Erskine Caldwell, Witter Bynner, William Saroyan, and William Carlos Williams. Villa's own stories quickly gained the attention of Edward J. O'Brien, who included him in several of his annual Best Short Stories

1. Villa numbered rather than titled most of his poems. The numbers bracketed throughout this essay follow the sequence in this new edition.

and dedicated the 1932 honor roll to him. In 1933, Scribner's published a collection of Villa's stories, *Footnote to Youth: Tales of the Philippines and Others*. The collection was generally seen as the work of a poetic temperament, with the *New York Times* noting that Villa "is essentially a poet who has, perhaps, chosen the wrong mode in which to express himself."

Indeed, shortly after *Footnote* saw print, Villa decided to concentrate on poetry. (For a time, the young writer had even considered a career as a painter. He would occasionally tell his workshop students that he had had a passion for painting but, unable to afford paint and canvas, dropped the brush in favor of the pen.) By 1933, according to his 1954 application for a Guggenheim Fellowship (which he received), "I delved intensively and extensively into English and American poetry, writing a great deal but not publishing any of my works at all." In retrospect, the defection was inevitable: the best of his stories declare the poet rather than the prose writer, serving as precursors to the poems.

When, in 1942, Viking Press published *Have Come, Am Here*, marking his American poetry debut, critical praise was immediate and generous. Writing in the *New York Times Book Review*, Peter Monro Jack described Villa's works as "an astonishing discovery . . . This is a poet of instinctive genius who creates knowingly his own communication." In a letter to B. W. Huebsch of Viking Press, the English writer Sylvia Townsend Warner—who, according to Villa, was the first person to whom he showed his poems—commented, "It is like seeing orchids growing wild to read him . . . Since I met him he seems to have met God; but a God so much in his own image that I am sure no harm can come of the encounter."

The influential critic Babette Deutsch anointed Villa in the *New Republic* in 1942 as part of a "small company of religious poets who have been able to communicate their vision. He belongs to the still smaller company of those who have not needed to cry out their doubt." Writing in the *Nation* that same year, Marianne Moore described the works as "bravely deep poems," where "final wisdom encountered in poem after poem merely serves to emphasize the disparity between tumult and stature."

Have Come, Am Here introduced a new method of rhyming that was mostly overlooked by reviewers—except for Deutsch, who included it in her *Poetry Handbook: A Dictionary of Terms*. Villa named his innovation "reversed consonance"—used in six of the poems—and explained in a note: "The last sounded consonants of the last syllable, or the last principal consonants of a word, are reversed for the corresponding rhyme. Thus, a rhyme for *near* would be *run*; or *rain, green, reign*. For *light—tell, tall, tale, steal*, etc." The opening lines of the first poem in both the original and this edition are a fine example:

It is what I never said,	(a)
What I'll always sing—	(b)
It's not found in days,	(a)
It's what always begins	(b)

Have Come is dedicated to Mark Van Doren and E. E. Cummings. The former judged the poems ready for publication when Villa, who had transferred to Columbia University where Van Doren was teaching, showed him the manuscript, while Cummings had written the aforementioned Mr. Huebsch: "It appears through a letter from Mr. Mark Van Doren that you'd like my confidential opinion of a certain manuscript. I very privately do not doubt that Vikings are blueeyed fools if they pass up José Garcia Villa's cargo." On publication of *Have Come, Am Here*, Cummings is reputed to have exclaimed, "and I am alive to find a brave man rediscovers the sky." By then, Cummings and Villa had been friends a little over a year, Villa a regular visitor to Patchin Place, where Cummings had his pied-à-terre in the Village. According to Villa's account, the two met because the younger poet wrote to Cummings faithfully, starting in 1938, shortly after he had read Cummings's *Collected Poems*. The book led to Villa's abandonment of the short story to "make poetry my *primary instrument*." Though Villa wrote Cummings yearly, the latter never replied until Villa wrote in 1941 "with the threat that, if he did not reply this time, I would *never* write to him again." This got the desired response: later that year Villa finally met the poet whose works had meant so much to him, the "man who opened up the world of poetry to me—without the inspiration of his work I probably would never have become a poet."

Volume Two followed in 1949, in which Villa introduced his "comma poems." In them, as he puts it, "the commas are an integral and essential part of the medium: regulating the poem's verbal density and time movement: enabling each word to attain a fuller tonal value, and the line movement to become more measured." The result, he says, is a "lineal pace of quiet dignity and movement," with the comma demanding to be, as it were, read between the words. It would be a mistake therefore to think the poems read the same way sans commas—a mistake predicated on the notion that only words can constitute a poem. (In this reissue, the usual space after the comma has been omitted in keeping with Villa's original design, which had been overlooked in *Volume Two* and, later, in *Selected Poems and New*.) To prove his point, Villa included comma-less versions of two poems. Here is the first stanza of one poem, with and without commas:

> Much,beauty,is,less,than,the,face,of,
> My,dark,hero. His,under,is,pure,
> Lightning. His,under,is,the,socket, [130]

> Much beauty is less than the face of
> My dark hero. His under is pure
> Lightning. His under is the socket [(130)]

The poet Richard Eberhart endorsed this unorthodox use of the comma, writing Villa on June 26, 1949:

> The arbitrary and perfectionist technique (so that not once does the machinery not click or work) of the comma is somehow, I don't know how, enlivening; it is a trick that refreshes, you know it is a trick and accept

it, and in spite of yourself you read right through the commas, so to speak . . . You do not employ trickery for trickery's sake, in verbal play, but your tricks are a delight to the eye and to the senses: plenty of sense to back up the startlingness.

Villa's last major publication was *Selected Poems and New*, in 1958. (There would be other books, notably *Parlement of Giraffes* and *Appassionata*, but these were mostly reprints of poems, chosen by Villa himself.) In her preface to *Selected Poems*, Edith Sitwell states, "I knew that I was seeing for the first time the work of a poet with a great, even an astonishing, and perfectly original gift," and that his works "are among some of the most beautiful written in our time."

That Villa succeeded in carving out a space for himself at a time when the New York literary scene was dominated by white writers is nothing short of amazing. A famous *Life* magazine photograph, taken in 1948 and much remarked upon, concretizes the Asian poet's arrival in Western literary circles. Celebrated British and American writers pose among the stacks of the Gotham Book Mart in Manhattan, among them Tennessee Williams, Marianne Moore, Elizabeth Bishop, Randall Jarrell, and, perched on a ladder, W. H. Auden. On Auden's right is Villa, peering out calmly at the world. In an essay published in the spring 2004 issue of *Melus*, "José Garcia Villa and Modernist Orientalism," Timothy Yu points out that American critics wanted to situate Villa "squarely in the Anglo American poetic canon"—just as the photo did—"satisfying Eliotic demands by positioning his individual talent with regard to a tradition," one that was then regarded as universal. Indeed, critics remarked on his influences, his antecedents, from the Metaphysical poets to Gerard Manley Hopkins, Walt Whitman, Emily Dickinson, and Cummings—all of whom the poet readily acknowledged, with pride of place given to E. E.

Is there an Orientalist subtext here? Perhaps; Yu certainly thinks so and argues, provocatively and with reason, that "the presence of Villa, an actual Asian subject, as a modernist writer

is quite a different kind of subversive Orientalism; he threatens
to overturn the Orientalist hierarchy at the heart of modernism,
in which classic Asian art and literature provide passive inspira-
tion to a vibrant Western modernism." There was certainly the
awareness that Villa was not native to these shores. For in-
stance, in a March 15, 1946, letter to Villa, after expressing ad-
miration for his poems, Henry Miller wrote, "What amazes
me, since you were born in the Philippines, is your deep grasp
of English." In her review cited earlier, Deutsch remarked:
"The fact that he is a native of the Philippines who comes to the
English language as a stranger may have helped him to his un-
usual syntax." Deutsch errs, of course, in believing Villa a
"stranger" to the English language—he was, like others of his
social class in Manila, multilingual, fluent in Tagalog, Spanish,
and English. It would be a mistake, however, to ascribe
Deutsch's comment to anything other than a case of plain igno-
rance, especially since Deutsch follows that observation with,
"But no accident of birth can account for his performance save
the ancient '*poeta nascitur, non fit.*' Even then the adage must
be qualified, for though he was undoubtedly born a poet, he has
obviously and wisely labored at his art."

Villa's English, as with that of writers in India and the Carib-
bean, was not the English of the colonial masters, but it was En-
glish nonetheless, or as critics of postcolonial literature describe
it, English with a small *e*. In claiming an imperial language as his
own—as such writers as Joseph Conrad and Vladimir Nabokov
had done—Villa demonstrated how linguistic ownership had
nothing to do with borders. There was an accent, sure, but it was
that of a prophet. Besides, the syntax of poetry is neither the syn-
tax of ordinary conversation nor that of prose. Villa's syntax
would have been unusual no matter what language he wrote in.
He was, after all, an unusual man, one who coined an unusual
name for himself: Doveglion—*dove, eagle,* and *lion.*

Villa's meteoric ascent is all the more remarkable given that
English had been present in the archipelago only since 1898—
brought over by Yankee soldiers during the Spanish-American
War, when the Americans easily divested a dying empire of its
sole Asian colony. The Yankees, however, had a harder time

convincing the islanders that the transfer, like so much chattel from old empire to new, was for the better. The reason was simple: Filipinos had risen against the Iberians in 1896—the first Asian revolution against a Western colonial power—and now, with a revolutionary government under Emilio Aguinaldo, had the Spanish on the ropes, trusting, rather naively, that the United States would help a long-oppressed people throw off their shackles. In a volte-face that betrayed its own revolutionary origins, the United States, as mandated by the 1898 Treaty of Paris, ultimately paid Spain $20 million for the Philippines, with Puerto Rico and Guam also placed under American control. But Filipino resistance was fierce, bloody, and long. The Philippine-American War broke out in 1899 and officially ended in 1902, though clashes in the interior continued for a decade. Grimmer than the better-known, three-month-long Spanish-American conflict, the Philippine-American War resulted in the loss of between at least a quarter of a million and a million mostly civilian lives, while American casualties amounted to more than four thousand dead.

The poet's father, Dr. Simeon Villa, had been General Aguinaldo's physician and chief of staff, with the rank of colonel; he did not look too kindly on either the Iberians or the North Americans. Or, for that matter, on his son's artistic calling. The old man wanted his son to follow him in his profession and also to manage their many real estate holdings in Ermita and Malate, Manila's fashionable districts. Villa did take medical courses at the University of New Mexico but quickly abandoned his stated goal of becoming a physician, to become, instead, a metaphysician, albeit in verse. In 1943, to the *New Yorker*'s "Talk of the Town," Villa quipped, "There is one thing a true poet can *not* do, and that is tickle frogs." His decision to be a full-time writer led Colonel Villa to gradually cut off all funds, leading to a permanent estrangement between father and son. In a letter written in Spanish and dated September 5, 1932, the colonel bemoans his prodigal son's spendthrift ways and castigates him: "If you return here, you will return naturally a *zero* (o). You left a *zero* and you will return a *zero*." On the rare occasion when the poet did speak of his father, it was always with considerable vitriol. I once asked Villa about the patriarch, whereupon he replied, "If I were to visit his grave, it would only be to spit on it!"

Villa's success in the metropolitan center—that of his country's colonizer, no less—elevated further his stature back home, to Olympian proportions. His contemporary, the writer Salvador P. Lopez, described the poet as "the one Filipino writer today who it would be futile to deride and impossible to ignore." In his introduction to *Poems by Doveglion* (1941), Lopez wrote that Doveglion is "a continuing vigorous influence in Filipino poetry, and that greatly increases his stature as a creative artist whose instrumental virtuosity, far from showing any signs of deterioration, can be seen to cut more cleanly and more deeply than before." Lopez, who believed art should possess a proletarian bent and therefore faulted Villa for his disregard of social realities, described Villa nonetheless as, according to Yu, "the patron saint of a cult of rebellious moderns." Even well into the 1970s, Villa acted as arbiter of what was praiseworthy in contemporary Philippine letters, inclusion in his selections regarded as virtual canonization. In 1973, he was named National Artist for Literature—one of the first awardees for the honor created by the Philippine government.

By then, a corresponding surge in nationalistic fervor, brought about by the repressive, conjugal dictatorship of Ferdinand Marcos and his wife Imelda (gleefully dubbed Queen Kong by Villa), had provoked a turn in Philippine literature toward realism and away from art for art's sake, whose chief proponent since the 1930s had been Villa. With "His" and "Hers" governments, the couple sought to legitimize martial law and their drive for dynastic power as necessary for the New Society, as they called their ostensibly brave remake of an oligarchic, semifeudal society into one that, by being responsive to the needs of the masses, would render superfluous a domestic Communist insurgency. Gilded and glittery, the idea of a New Society was in the end really a fig leaf for unabashed personal ambition.

In such an atmosphere, when armed revolution was a distinct

possibility, many of the Manila literati considered Villa irrelevant. But, in "Conversations with José Garcia Villa," in a 1979 issue of the now-defunct Manila journal *Archipelago*, poet Cirilo Bautista argues that there were other writers who "looked back to his work in search of an approach to their artistic problem concerning the functional utility of their poetry in the face of the changes being introduced by the New Society. In short, they were re-learning from him, seeking in his work certain aspects that they might have overlooked or ignored earlier."

Villa's strategic placement, combined with his eccentric but formidable poetic gifts, helped propel Philippine literature in English out of the swamps of late-nineteenth-century romanticism straight into modernity. Yet his own work, even at its most ascetic, always hints at a full-blooded, albeit quirky, romantic—the sensual animal proud beneath the priestly robes. It is this tension between the sensual and the spiritual that marks his sensibility, an assertion on the literary landscape that was unique, startlingly lyrical, and unapologetically devoid of many of the hallmarks of American poetic modernity; e.g., the conversational tone, the attention paid to the details of quotidian life, the confessional, the unremarkable first line. The external world held little interest for Villa the poet—one didn't read him to get the "news," and its lack in his lines was revivifying. If anything, the life evinced by his poems was almost completely interiorized, full of what Hopkins would have termed "inscapes," a world where the poet proclaims, "Clean,like,iodoform,between,the,tall, / Letters,of,*Death*,I,see,Life . . ." [143] and where the stratagems of a woman's faith involve:

> A fleet of angels, satin-shod;
> They kiss like angels, every one,
> And poison like an inverted God. [77]

Villa had no fashionable cause to advance or defend except that of poetry itself. In his hands it evolves into a mighty engine of flight, winged with an exacting spiritual and aesthetic vision and an abundant lyrical gift honed by a keen critical intelligence. Because his poetic sensibility disavows any commingling with that of prose, his works arrive at a nondeclarative, even mystical, meaning, circumventing the prosy pitfalls of narrative to thereby retain a strict poetic purity. His visions can only be uttered in a poet's tongue, and *only* in *his* tongue. They are indeed strange, as anyone speaking in tongues would sound strange, but it is this very strangeness that renders them both astonishing and compelling.

Whenever the poet takes notice of the world, or of certain elements in it, that world, those elements, are seen not for themselves—for in themselves they are unknowable—but as reflections of an imagination that can be surreal: "A radio made of seawater / Will have mermaids for music:" [45]. Or consider these painterly lines, from a poem that Samuel Barber set to music in 1944: "I have observed pink monks eating blue raisins. / And I have observed blue monks eating pink raisins" [42].

Villa constantly polished his craft, so that his language entertains and illuminates mind, ear, and psyche—qualities rarely seen in the dreary, earnest products churned out by today's poetry mills. Frequently quoting Mallarmé's dictum to his students, that poetry "is written not with ideas but with words," Villa would routinely point to poems in the *New Yorker* as exemplifying failed poetry, or poetry that never graduated from prose—a charge he would still, I am certain, level against that otherwise exemplary magazine, whose cartoons he cherished and often used to illustrate his points.

He believed fervently in a first line that grabbed the reader's attention. Without that initial lapel-grabber—what he termed "the coiled cobra"—the poem limps along, unable to vault forward. Once hooked, the reader continues, but the challenge for the poet is to ensure that succeeding lines sustain the initial burst of linguistic energy. Here is a lovely example of how, seemingly effortlessly, the opening line flows into the rest of the stanza:

> Be beautiful, noble, like the antique ant,
> Who bore the storms as he bore the sun,
> Wearing neither gown nor helmet,
> Though he was archbishop and soldier:
> Wore only his own flesh. [39]

He was equally insistent that the natural pauses dictated by breath, while valid, were the least interesting means of enjambment. In a 1982 interview with Manila professor and critic Doreen Fernandez, he had this to say: "When your breath pauses, [the line] stops. There is no craft there. Any ignorant person can write like that; a child can write like that . . . Art is craft before it is meaning." It took craft to control the musical flow, from line to line, from stanza to stanza. And even within the line, a poet could regulate movement and tone through, for instance, Villa's Duo-Technique—an innovation John Edwin Cowen, his literary trustee and former student, explains, along with poetic aphorisms Villa called Xocerisms (some of which are included here), in an editor's note at the end of this book.

Those may find him difficult, then, who expect of poetry convenient homilies, the exposition of ideas, narrative meaning, and self-expression. He is cerebral but also celebratory and witty, especially in his aphorisms; e.g., "Skies,are,written / Because, poems,are,born" and "The,pleasure,of,history, / Is,its,knack,of, being,late: / To,arrive,a,ghost: / Or,the,metaphysics,of,success." Especially in his Divine Poems, his work pays homage to the mystery of being while speaking its language:

> When,I,was,no,bigger,than,a,huge,
> Star,in,my,self,I,began,to,write,
> My,
> Theology,
> Of,rose,and,
>
> Tiger: . . . [134]

In "The Anchored Angel," in my estimation a great poem, we witness a peerless musicality, muscular language, startling imagery, and a fusion of transcendent and erotic love. Here is the opening stanza:

> And,lay,he,down,the,golden,father,
> (Genesis',fist,all,gentle,now)
> Between,the,wall,of,China,and,

> The,tiger,tree (his,centuries,his,
> Aerials,of,light) . . .
>   Anchored,entire,angel!
> He,in,his,estate,miracle,and,living,dew,
> His,fuses,gold,his,cobalts,love,
>   And,in,his,eyepits,
> O,under,the,liontelling,sun—
> The,zeta,truth—the,swift,red,Christ. [190]

The poem ends with the stunning and iconoclastic portrait of a complete Messiah: "Through,whose,huge,discalced,arable, love, / Bloodblazes,oh,Christ's,gentle,egg: His,terrific,sperm."

The Divine Poems call forth a metaphysical realm in which God needs us as much as we need God. To paraphrase Voltaire, if one didn't exist, the other would have had to invent him. The Villa-esque Divine and Supreme Being differs from the God of, say, John Donne, an overwhelming force that clearly can dispense with humanity. When Donne writes, "Batter me, three-person'd God . . . ," he assumes a supplicant's pose. In contrast, Villa's relationship with God is intimate and familial. Poem 60, where the poet and God joust, ends on a fraternal note:

> Then He pushes me and I plunge down, down!
> And when He comes to help me up
> I put my arms around Him, saying, "Brother,
> Brother." . . . This is the way we are.

Humanizing God at the same time that he renders the human divine, the poet enables us to view God as a historical rather than ahistorical primal force. Villa's God, with whom he wrestles, argues, talks, and plays, could be reasonably interpreted as the idea of America, a kind of promised land where the poet could find liberation from an oppressive society and a domineering father, to replace—though never completely—Old World / Old Testament contexts with New World / New Testament ones. It is a relationship that is not only paternal but, as I have pointed out, fraternal as well, with ironic echoes of that patronizing phrase, "little brown brothers," with which American colonial administrators described Filipinos. America needed Villa the poet to ground itself in human values, a partnership that erects a "kinetic balance and dignity" and allows the man/poet to take aim at the Fountainhead with a bow and arrow. When asked why, he declares:

> "I will not
>   Murder thee! I do but
> Measure thee. Hold
>
> Thy peace." And this I did.
> But I was curious
>   Of this so regal head.
> "Give thy name"—"Sir! Genius!" [49]

My hope is that, on the centennial of his birth, this reissuance of José Garcia Villa's poems will accelerate the growing revival of interest in his work. There is no question that he deserves a place in the pantheon of American literature, a fact Conrad Aiken recognized when he included eight of Villa's works in his 1944 Modern Library anthology, *Twentieth-Century American Poetry*. Sadly, most current American poetry anthologies exclude him, rendering this Penguin edition all the more valuable.

And he belongs as well to the pantheon of Asian American literature. Prior to Juliana Chang's 1996 anthology, *Quiet Fire*, Asian American poetry collections simply ignored him—he is, for instance, glaringly absent from the landmark 1974 anthology *AIIIEEEEE!*, while his contemporary Carlos Bulosan, who wrote mesmerizingly on the travails of the Filipino immigrant, was included, and rightfully so. It is true that Villa deliberately avoided any references to his ethnicity, or to his own experience as a person of color in the United States (though in private he complained about being paid less than other writing instructors at the New School and at one point contemplated taking legal action). Taken to task for his insistent desire to be regarded as "universal"—he was, after all, a creature of his age—wherein "universal" was synonymous with the Western tradition, still he felt no obligation to display in his art overt signs of his situation in the world, believing that that was irrelevant and, moreover, lay in the province of prose.

Clearly, political correctness trumped literature, the argument being that if Villa didn't care for such a category, why should its self-appointed guardians care for him? This is not an argument of course but a snub, and for ill-conceived reasons, unwittingly reinforcing the way in which the mainstream has historically boxed in, or ghettoized, writers of color. Contemporary Asian American poets, thankfully insistent on their full rights as citizens of the republic of poetry, are as likely to write on topics that have nothing to do with their historical condition as they are to dwell on it. In this, too, Villa was a pioneer.

In the end, what should matter most is what mattered to Villa: the words themselves, unmediated except by the reader's own perceptions. Villa's music, language, imagery, and versification mesh in a totality that is deeply pleasurable and magical, with an adamantine beauty that simultaneously cuts and illuminates. These poems ensorcell, and I have no doubt they will ensorcell for a very long time to come.

My heartfelt thanks to David Joel Friedman, Eugene Gloria, and John Edwin Cowen—fine poets all—for their insightful comments on this introduction as it was taking shape. Additionally, John, as Villa's literary trustee, provided me with copies of relevant material such as letters and reviews that proved indispensable in contextualizing Villa's creations.

LUIS H. FRANCIA
New York City

Suggestions for Further Reading

The Anchored Angel: Selected Writings by José García Villa. Edited by Eileen Tabios. New York: Kaya, 1999.

The Critical Villa: Essays in Literary Criticism by José García Villa. Edited by Jonathan Chua. Manila: Ateneo de Manila University Press, 2002.

The Parlement of Giraffes: Poems for Children—Eight to Eighty. Edited by John Cowen. With original drawings by Villa. Tagalog translation by Larry Francia. Manila: Anvil, 1999.

EDITED BY VILLA

Bravo: The Poet's Magazine. Founded by Villa in 1980 and still published by Bravo Editions, New York.

A Celebration for Edith Sitwell. New York: New Directions, 1948.

Clay: A Literary Notebook. Published at the University of New Mexico in Albuquerque in 1931.

"Cummings Number." *The Harvard Wake* 5 (Spring 1946).

Introducing Mr. Vanderborg: Poems by Arthur Vanderborg. New York: King and Cowen, 1977.

"Marianne Moore Issue." *Quarterly Review of Literature* (1948).

The New Doveglion Book of Philippine Poetry. 3rd ed. Manila: Anvil, 1994.

CONTRIBUTIONS IN ANTHOLOGIES
(CITATIONS FROM 1970 TO 2008)

Chang, Juliana, ed. *Quiet Fire: A Historical Anthology of Asian American Poetry, 1892–1970*. New York: Asian American Writers' Workshop, 1996.

Chang, Tina, Nathalie Handal, and Ravi Shankar, eds. *Language for a New Century: Contemporary Poetry from the Middle East, Asia, and Beyond*. New York and London: W. W. Norton & Co., 2008.

Cline, Jay, et al. *New Voices 4*. Lexington, MA: Ginn, 1978.

Cowen, John Edwin. *English Teacher's Portfolio of Multicultural Activities*. West Nyack, NY: Center for Applied Research in Education, 1996.

Dato, R., P. Laslo, and Carlos Bulosan, eds. *Early Poets (1909–1942)*. Manila: A. S. Florentino, 1973.

Day, A. Grove, ed. *The Art of Narration: The Short Story*. New York: McGraw-Hill, 1971.

Elements of Writing. Pupil's Edition and Annotated Teacher's Edition. Holt, 1993.

Exploring Poetry. CD-ROM. Detroit: Gale Research, 1996.

Francia, H. S., Jr., ed. *Poems, Paintings, and Graphics by Twenty Filipino Artists*. Manila: Balthazar, 1971.

Francia, Luis H., ed. *Brown River, White Ocean: An Anthology of Twentieth-Century Philippine Literature in English*. New Brunswick, NJ: Rutgers University Press, 1993.

Garrigue, Jean, ed. *Love's Aspects: The World's Great Love Poems*. Garden City, NY: Doubleday, 1975.

Gross, Theodore. *A Nation of Nations: Ethnic Literature in America*. New York: Free Press, 1971.

Hagedorn, Jessica, ed. *Charlie Chan Is Dead: An Anthology of Contemporary Asian American Fiction*. New York: Penguin, 1993, 2004.

Hodgins, Francis, and Kenneth Silverman, eds. *Adventures in American Literature*. Heritage edition. Orlando, FL: Harcourt Brace, 1985.

Hsu, Kai-yu, and Helen Palubinskas, eds. *Asian-American Authors*. Boston: Houghton Mifflin, 1972.

Hufana, Alex, ed. *Philippine Writings: Short Stories, Essays, and Poetry with German Contributions on Philippine Literature*. Manila: Regal, 1977.

Kennedy, X. J., and Dorothy M. Kennedy, eds. *Knock at a Star: A Child's Introduction to Poetry*. Boston: Little, Brown, 1982.

Kostelanetz, Richard, ed. *Text-Sound Texts*. New York: William Morrow, 1980.

Language and Composition. Pupil's and Teacher's Editions. New York: Harcourt Brace, 1990.

Laslo, P., ed. *English-German Anthology of Filipino Poets*. 3rd ed. Manila: A. S. Florentino, 1973.

Levy, Paul, ed. *The Penguin Book of Food and Drink*. London: Viking, 1996.

McFarland, P., Frances Feagin, et al. *Forms in English Literature*. Boston: Houghton Mifflin, 1978.

Newman, Katharine, ed. *The American Equation: Literature in Multi-Ethnic Culture*. Boston: Allyn and Bacon, 1971.

Prentice-Hall Literature. Teacher's and Student's Annotated Editions. Englewood Cliffs, NJ: Prentice-Hall, 1993.

Realuyo, Bino A., ed. *The NuyorAsian Anthology*. New York: Asian American Writers' Workshop, 1999.

Rothenberg, Jerome, and George Quasha, eds. *America a Prophecy*. New York: Random House, 1973.

Santaromana, M. L., ed. *Sinaglahi*. Quezon City: Writers Union of the Philippines, 1975.

Villa, José Garcia. *55 Poems*. Selected and translated into Tagalog by Hilario S. Francia Jr., Quezon City: University of the Philippines, 1988.

Washburn, Katharine, and John S. Major, eds. *World Poetry: An Anthology of Verse from Antiquity to Our Time*. Clifton Fadiman, general editor. New York and London: W. W. Norton, 1998.

Zapanta-Manlapaz, Edna, and Gémino H. Abad, comps. *Index*

to *Filipino Poetry in English, 1905–1950.* Manila: National Book Store, 1988.

————, eds. *Man of Earth: An Anthology of Filipino Poetry and Verse from English, 1905 to the Mid-50s.* Quezon City: Ateneo de Manila University Press, 1989.

A Note on the Text

This Centennial Edition celebrating the birth of poet José Garcia Villa, aka Doveglion, on August 5, 1908, collects the best poems written and published by Villa in his lifetime, including the complete 1942 publication of Viking/Penguin's *Have Come, Am Here*, the poet's first U.S. book of poems. All of the poems from *Selected Poems and New* (1958) appear here, including Villa's designated poems from *Volume Two* (1949) and thirty-one previously unpublished U.S. poems from *Appassionata: Poems in Praise of Love* (1979). Also appearing for the first time are Villa's versification innovation (Duo-Technique), his new adaptations, and witty, brilliant aphorisms (Xocerisms) on sex/love, God, poetry, et cetera, which in Villa's words are "pithy, philosophical insights told with a dash of Tabasco."

JEC

Doveglion: Collected Poems

HAVE COME, AM HERE

(1942)

LYRICS: I

It is what I never said,
What I'll always sing—
It's not found in days,
It's what always begins
In half dark, in half light.
It's shining so curved
Yet rises so tall and tells
Where the first flower dove
When God's hands lost love.
It's a great word without sound
Without echo to reveal
Where fragrance went down!
O, but it's all of it there
Above my poems a Wreath.

2

There was a time
Where it was always deep:
This place was always punctual
Because it was a rose.

This was the rose
Where always Truth died,
At whose silver side
An angel always denied.

This was only I
Wandering deep, so deep!
And death was always punctual
Because I had a beautiful skull.

3

When the pigeon walked toward me,
Suddenly his breast burst open:
God was there in the wound
Walking to me!

Nearer he came and nearer,
Pigeon and God together;
At the base of my mortal body
Looking up at me!

Gesturing to me without motion,
Talking to me without words:
"Open. Open. Let me ascend.
Open. Open!"

Then did I will my body to break,
To break, to break, for Door!
And God leapt in and rose
Fire in my realms of bone.

4

Nobody yet knows who I am,
Nor myself may;
Nor yet what I deal,
Nor yet where I lead.

But in my skull already bright,
And death in rose attire,
And in my mouth already star
And jewels firmly wrought.

And in my eyes a sweetness
Almost fierce as the sun,
And in my ears already music
Hearing the future kiss.

Yet myself knows myself not,
Is it I have forgotten?
Yet Finality is very near—
I rush, I run, I run!

5

O the Eyes that will see me,
And the Mouth that will kiss me.
And the Rose I will stand on,
And the Hand that will turn me.

This will be in a Time of mirrors.

O the Tiger that will point me,
And the Light that will drown me.
And the Voice that will sing me,
And the God I will dethrone.

This is the Death I will stand on.

6

I will break God's seamless skull,
And I will break His kissless mouth,
O I'll break out of His faultless shell
And fall me upon Eve's gold mouth.

I will pound against His skull,
I will crack it by my force of love:
I'll be a cyclone gale and spill
Me out of His bounding groove.

I'll be upon Eve, upon Eve,
Upon Eve and her coasts of love!
I'll be upon Eve, upon Eve,

Cataract of Adamhood. There would I be
My Lord! there would I rebuild me Thee
There alone find my Finality.

7

Between God's eyelashes I look at you,
Contend with the Lord to love you,
In this house without death I break His skull
I ache, I ache to love you.

I will batter God's skull God's skull God's skull!
I will batter it till He love you
And out of Him I'll dash I'll dash
To thy coasts, O mortal flesh.

He'll be broken He'll be broken He'll be broken
By my force of love He'll be broken
And when I reach your side O Eve
You'll break me you'll break me you'll break me.

8

As in a rose the true fire moves,
As in a fire the true mind lives,
I beheld in a rose the eyes
That in their pure force swung

My bells, my voice, my heart
The spirit and the lovely thews
The bones and the lovely skull—
Into the eternity structural.

Eternity has a structure great
Only the rose's eyes may meet:
The operant beams are set
Where none but flame may live:
A magnitude of spermal love
In a plasm death-devout:
Structured thus, within a rose's eyes I saw
The rigors of immortal law.

9

It's a hurricane of spirit—
That's genius! Not God can tear
It from itself, though He is the rose
In this skull that's seer.
Skull revolving rose: that's I!
I am in my skull and spy
Eternity and Now and Why.

It's a mastery of death—
And that's Love. It's the bequeathèd
Mind of Christ. It's I, it's Love,
What the great deaths reveal.
I revolve a skull, I rose!
I revolve a skull that knows
I make it speak God's voice!

10

O three eyen hath God:
One rose and
Two wounded hands:

Three shadows hath
His rose
One shadow His three eyes:

His two wounded hands
Shadowless
And this unshadow is Love.

11

When I shall the first time seek my Life
O God's three eyen shall burnen me,
Till my clothes begin to fail
And I His beginning nude am made.

That first time shall burnen me
His three eyen shall piercen me!
Till at last my eyes in shreds
I my beginning Life shall see.

Yet perished thus by His eyen three,
I a Nude and He my eyes!
Deft my spiritual fingers weave
Love the incomparable Life.

12

Leaned in my eyes and loved me.
Leaned in my throat and spoke.
Dared my grovelling bloodscape,
It to a dazzeling diamond made.

Thighed me to its lust of light!
Thrust me to its deep of pride!
Blocked the only mortal door
Where Anonymity in might steal:

Leaned, dared, thighed, thrust,
Blocked my descending dust!

13

There is a one that createth me,
He that of me is my sun my sum
My father and my only child:—
Behold—we do wander, wonder
Which of us is the uplifted candle,
Which of us will read, will rede
The image of our living shadow;
O there's a breath of us will live,
There's a Third of us will dive
Out of the Light, out of the Wooed,
Into eternity dazzling dark:
O but here shall turn, shall spring
The Word young, young, blue-eyed yet,
Slender as an infant fawn and
Whole without death's antlers yet.

14

am so very am and
speak so very speak
and look my every hand
is for each all lovers' sake

and nowherever time
can farther never go
tomorrow can not climb
over each least lover's brow

my every vein rings
now's lifest rose: my skull
is among the kings
in that danger steeple

where each air breathed
is a love to glow to sing
and each love wreathed
is but God's beginning

because He can not be
until Am is Am in flame
fire is His dancing augury
to give love His name

15

When the world shall come to its end
On the world's last Love I'll stand.
O God will try to push me down but I
With all my force will push Him back.

He shall not be able to put out Love at all.
O I'll guard it, guard it, guard it!
And the world cannot die with Love glowing, burning,
O the world cannot die out at all.

Doomsday will be shattered, shattered!
Shattered by my standing there:
God will see whom He is contending with
And, O, He'll revolve the world again.

16

In my desire to be Nude
I clothed myself in fire:—
Burned down my walls, my roof,
Burned all these down.

Emerged myself supremely lean
Unsheathed like a holy knife.
With only His Hand to find
To hold me beyond annul.

And found Him found Him found Him
Found the Hand to hold me up!
He held me like a burning poem
And waved me all over the world.

LYRICS: II

17

First, a poem must be magical,
Then musical as a sea-gull.
It must be a brightness moving
And hold secret a bird's flowering.
It must be slender as a bell,
And it must hold fire as well.
It must have the wisdom of bows
And it must kneel like a rose.
It must be able to hear
The luminance of dove and deer.
It must be able to hide
What it seeks, like a bride.
And over all I would like to hover
God, smiling from the poem's cover.

18

She has gone,
Who was ever alone.
I am left a haunted
Land. But mounted
Upon my brow a star
Henceforth to unbar
All mystery of such
As she whose much-
Ness must stand
Alone in any land.
Music has passed
By me and surpassed

Love. No limb's fire
Can ever aspire
To hold her. Body
Of love insuffices di-
Vinity of loneliness.
She must be loveless
And merely haunt.
Blessèd I, once at her font.

19

I can no more hear Love's
Voice. No more moves
The mouth of her. Birds
No more sing. Words
I speak return lonely.
Flowers I pick turn ghostly.
Fire that I burn glows
Pale. No more blows
The wind. Time tells
No more truth. Bells
Ring no more in me.
I am all alone singly.
Lonely rests my head.
—O my God! I am dead.

20

I can not speak of the beauty of love
Without wonder. It is my belief of spring

That makes music invincible and poetry
A thing of goldest green. If I can not

Touch her thighs I shall nevermore sing
And birds will nevermore speak. It is this

Truth alone that keeps Jesu to go on. And
He is most lonely but the thought of me

And my love and my songs, these, like
Distant music, yes, these keep him going on.

21

And if the heart can not love
death can not cure it nor sleep
nor splendor of wound the heart
has no sound

Bloom has escaped it and
birth the miraculous flower
and music and speech leave
it unbewitched

God it can not spell nor sun
nor lover the beautiful word
and it has no sound no sound
nor wound

22

I was speaking of oranges to a lady
of great goodness when O the lovely

giraffes came. Soon it was all their
splendor about us and my throat

ached with the voice of great larks.
O the giraffes were so beautiful as

if they meant to stagger us by such
overwhelming vision: Let us give

each a rose said my beautiful lady
of great goodness and we sent the

larks away to find roses. It was
while the larks were away that

the whitest giraffe among them
and the goldest one among them

O these two loveliest ones sought
and found us: bent before us two

kneeling with their divine heads
bowed. And it was then we knew

why all this loveliness was sent
us: the white prince and the golden

princess kneeling: to adore us
brightly: we the Perfect Lovers.

23

Girl singing. Day. And on her way
She has to pass by the oldest mountain.
That at least is certain. Rain. That
Doth leave no stain. And again whose
Flowers move jealously. O pity me.
O if her eyes move and destroy all
Firmament. How brightly devised is
That moment. Much and muchly praised.
O day imperishably dazed. O woman
God-grazed. Succour God alone, O
Teach him Joy. O girl singing. O
For whom alone God bows out. O lovely
Throat. O world's end. O brightly
Devised crystal moment.

24

O Lovely. O lovely as panther. O
Creation's supremest dissenter.
Enter. Teach me thy luminous ire.
O jewelled, pacing, night-displacing
Fire. O night's nimble-dancing, No-
Saying lyre. Embrace me. Defy me.
Reave me. None shall defend me.
Not God. Not I. Purify me. Consume
Me. Disintegrate me to thy ecstasy.
O lovely and without mercy. O dark-
Footed divinity. O Lovely and Terrible.
O Death-irreducible. O Unimpeachable.

25

There came you wishing me * * *
And so I said * * *
And then you turned your head
With the greatest beauty

Smiting me mercilessly!
And then you said * * *
So that my heart was made
Into the strangest country . . .

* * * you said, so beauteously,
So that an angel came
To hear that name,
And we caught him tremulously!

26

Hands handle the hours of night
More than the day's.

Hands and a weapon.
Triune bright-resolute
While Death stares mute.
Death is overpowered
By this pure power.
These are the hands and the weapon
Of a Master.
Triune bright-resolute
The hands kiss God:
He ionizes hands and weapon.
Triune bright-resolute
Trinite of utmost love—
Advance—advance!

27

her day-rose is much sweet
her kisses are most love
such kissness is not told
withouten her rose's fold

but birds bees best lovers
brave lovers aseeken more
a seekness as of God's word
their loverness hath sword

for girlshape has girlgraces
of day-rose and night-rose
though day-rose be much sweet
yet night-rose is sevenly sweet

there where her night begins
there be her goldest rosest rose
that in her deep wisdom knows
boygrace will knight her Rose

O there where her night begins
there be her wondrous wondrous rose

O withouten her night-rose
I be forlornly aloss aloss

28

Am.
        —But if being God has made
you fear and taught you terror—
if in this very deepest final mirror
Time has concentred the horrible shade

of extremest Tree under extremest Sun:

O Burning Laurel—
                        if in this most
deathless altitude comes the ghost
with the sure, well-levelled gun—

Nay do not bend. Be mostly tall—
arise to thy perfect height, be
equal to Terror's proud solemnity
that, aiming for thy fall,

pulls her trigger but proves her bullet
blank against an unconquerable Target.

29

Silence is Thought converging,
Unprecipitate, like
Dancer on tight wire balancing,
Transitive, budlike,

Till—her act finished—in
One lovely jump skips
She to the floor, bending
To make her bows, dips

Herself in bright applause—
Then silence is
No more. Now it is the rose
Called Speech.

30

I did sternly (why not) ask very Death
to die, pointing my finger fiery
at him.
        Death held his pirate breath.
I did (then) assume my (God's) livery
urging all immortality's guard (my
angels) to help Death die
with gallant bravery.

Death bowed uncowed: "I cannot
die
     though (yes) that I would
having lived too long in the Dark Wood

I seek Light, Light, the God-Begot

yet thou (God) not having sired me
my scythe supersedes my gallantry."

31

By all the luminance of her voice I swear
(and wine is not more wise than whose roses)
sing to me who tigers so musically discover

(deeply) about the bright limbs' pauses.

When in such light—(though it be darkly, so
beautifully, silently night) my Eden sword
his rose-immortal war halts (briefly) to hoard

the luminous word: the only equal of the foe—

Then do I behold such tigers as more
brilliantly move than the Lord's archangels,
Crouching fair, stripèd, at the very door

of Heaven: Damoclean princes with bells
of fire all ready to loose and peal
—to me, mortal—the Word—and so I spill.

32

than whose roses. And if her love be musical
as star more proudly moves than water
being by God's cause her diviner sister
move then to me brightly her body's vessel
and all its secrecies and all its dangers
than whose roseness there is no equal
but I, lone emperor of the gentlest tigers
the limbs' wild music, strange and beautiful.

I am more than God's equal—I am Love's
most equal. I am he that moves to kiss
her very soul, her very deep: who weaves
of her the bright banner of immortality's
most honor. I am he that through her shuttles
:Lover, divinest Lover: Father, Creator of
                                        Immortal Battles.

LYRICS: III

33

I think, yes, a leopard in Dufy blue would
Be incomparable. Provided his eyes are green
And see death like two flowers. Myself would

Bring him me all in dazzling gold. Lie
At his feet for God's sake awaiting death. The
Blue paw will have its incomparable law. The

Green eyes incomparable words. What voice
This blue this green can muster is weight of
Immensest love. And I am love myself awaiting

This immensity. O fall quick, pure feet, pure
Eyes. Fall heavy, immortal leopard. Par death
Lift me, compare me to your incomparability.

34

Bring the pigeons watermelons, Abelard.
The order has cool philosophic purity.
This is not largesse but Roman nobility.

Bring the peacocks oranges.
Turn the philosophy to sensuousness.
Pallas Athene is Greek thereby.

But if we bring the watermelons pigeons?
If we bring the oranges peacocks?
Is that very difficult?

This would not be Greek nor Roman.
This would be purity without philosophy.
This would be artistry.

35

Inviting a tiger for a weekend.
The gesture is not heroics but discipline.
The memoirs will be splendid.

Proceed to dazzlement, Augustine.
Banish little birds, graduate to tiger.
Proceed to dazzlement, Augustine.

Any tiger of whatever colour
The same as jewels any stone
Flames always essential morn.

The guest is luminous, peer of Blake.
The host is gallant, eye of Death.
If you will do this you will break

The little religions for my sake.
Invite a tiger for a weekend,
Proceed to dazzlement, Augustine.

36

The distinction is in Fire and Division:
Ferocious and beautiful Leopard that thrives
On the rose-imagination.

Supreme visionary Guard begetting poetry:
Magnetizer to Confrontation till the archives
Cry in luminosity.

Break the heart's thicketry, leap, Leopard-mind,
Bring figuration of Fire. Great Geometer, design
The death assigned

Austerely rose but austerely fire. Let expire
Upon the frailest terrible line
The Phoenix's desire.

37

Take a very straight line, Fermin, if you want to die.
The line at the middle of fire, that is.
So that it is perpendicular, central.

Die illuminist, Fermin, rising and particular.
Cohere at the electric center of death.
Ascend the incandescent rope and throw

Your tenderness to me below. If they call you buffoon,
Fermin, I have violins to drown them out—
But you have a Confrontation to make.

38

Now I prize yellow strawberries—
With their dignities of silk and
Their archbishpal opulence—
Rivalling God the peacock only.

Assuming neither space nor time,
A purely intellectual fruit,
Yet of matchless elegance. This
Is my intellectual religion.

For I would not have bishops lean
Nor peacocks irreligious, but

Temper them to that great gold pitch
Of the first-ascending bridegroom.

So, to the tune of yellow strawberries,
Announce to philosophy my arrival—
O a little irreverent perhaps
But religiously, peerlessly musical.

39

Be beautiful, noble, like the antique ant,
Who bore the storms as he bore the sun,
Wearing neither gown nor helmet,
Though he was archbishop and soldier:
Wore only his own flesh.

Salute characters with gracious dignity:
Though what these are is left to
Your own terms. Exact: the universe is
Not so small but these will be found
Somewhere. Exact: they will be found.

Speak with great moderation: but think
With great fierceness, burning passion:
Though what the ant thought
No annals reveal, nor his descendants
Break the seal.

Trace the tracelessness of the ant,
Every ant has reached this perfection.
As he comes, so he goes,
Flowing as water flows,
Essential but secret like a rose.

40

In Picasso you see Blue, Rose, and the
Virginity of Cubes. The sound of his colors
Is autumn. The melancholy of apricots
Hang like Chagall angels above each picture.
This man is Milton gay, very sad.

And though he paints no angels, the nudes
Are tragic like them. Very silent bells
Ring requiem. The cubes are cubes of grief.
But being virgins the cubes spring alert.
But the nudes are silent, being unvirgins.

It takes tenderness to perceive: for the colors,
The nudes, the cubes to afflict. Unless
One were versed in the tauromachy of art.
Then persuasion is instant: you lie fallen,
Victor, gripping great, very sad horns.

LYRICS: IV

41

To make icecream chrysantheme
Mix Christ and chrysanthemums

In a bowl of turkiz amethyst.
To make icecream chrysantheme.

But since Christ is not so easy
(You must hunt him first among

The white shadows of black birds
With a mask upon your shoulder

And a rose upon your eyes!)—
Since Christ is not so easy

If you come Christless from the
Hunt, though chrysanthemums be

Gold and bright as poems, and
Carry hugest themes—naught

Can they avail, ah they will fail,
And then your lips must say

Goodbye, goodbye, goodbye
To icecream chrysantheme.

42

I have observed pink monks eating blue raisins.
And I have observed blue monks eating pink raisins.
Studiously have I observed.

Now, this is the way a pink monk eats a blue raisin:
Pink is he and it is blue and the pink
Swallows the blue. I swear this is true.

And the way a blue monk eats a pink raisin is this:
Blue is he and it is pink and the blue
Swallows the pink. And this also is truth.

Indeed I have observed and myself have partaken
Of blue and pink raisins. But my joy was different:
My joy was to see the blue and the pink counterpointing.

43

roses racing with rabbits

around my favorite church
(nowhere) yet we will all

go there (I love you, with
roses and rabbits and roses

I love you) we will climb
the beautiful steeple and

watch (perhaps ring bells
whose bells who knows)

but in the secret unmercy
of all this beauty, O

you will open your eyes
upon certainly somewhere

around God's heart (every-
where O everywhere) but

most certainly and mostly
look, Loren, look! my heart.

44

sky wrote me blackbirds

that were gold (perhaps God
laughing, strolling upside down)
I replied,
                    Impossible
                              even for
a miracle! Then God
strolling upside down (perhaps
roses skiing)
                    said,
                              Possible
We (Love and I) saw dwarfs
in Mars, and a marriage
of lemons
                    in the house
of peace . . .
                    And forthwith
I believed and with God I
went laughing, arm in arm
strolling upside down

45

A radio made of seawater
Will have mermaids for music:

Who when me they will kiss
All my senses will greet.

A radio made of birds
Will have music of grapes!
Who between their ribs
Shall carry joys without peer.

But a radio made of Light
Will have music of Blakes:
Who with great tigertails
Will beat God-musicales.

46

in blue without when blues dream bears
the only living girls are gold
quickly the living boys will bring them stars
and stars will sing them bells

in bells without when bells dream blooms
the only living boys are brave
quickly the living girls will bring them dooms
and dooms will praise their love

47

All the horses were gold.
All their hooves could deal
Death. Yet me they dealt sun.
With what tenderness
The gold horses loved me!
For my eyes they made
Dignity, for my heart
The fadeless final star.
Love they brought also

But without the sorrow seal.
With their eyes they spoke me
The love God could never make.
These horses so beautiful
I could wish to trample my life!
But sun they brought me,
O their hooves would not smite.

DIVINE POEMS

48

If my sun set in the west
I could not bear it!
And if it rose in the east—
I must annul it!
Myself demands
Rarest Circuit.

'Twere natural history
To set in the west,—
But my sun's imperialcy
Hath this reversed,—
To reach all Lands
Exquisite and first.

49

God said, "I made a man
Out of clay—
    But so bright he, he spun
Himself to brightest Day

Till he was all shining gold,
And oh,
    He was lovely to behold!
But in his hands held he a bow

Aimed at me who created
Him. And I said,
    'Wouldst murder me
Who am thy Fountainhead!'

Then spoke he the man of gold:
'I will not
    Murder thee! I do but
Measure thee. Hold

Thy peace.' And this I did.
But I was curious
    Of this so regal head.
'Give thy name!'—'Sir! Genius.'"

50

Countering the general eye,
To surpass it quietly,
These eyes stay in private sockets

To detect the invisible currents
Whose metrics is immortality.
In consequence whereof,

These lines are charged
With ions heretic! O do not touch
Here unless you are prepared

Or can sustain the hidden
Voltage. Move away, gaze away,
Or yield the Self gracefully too.

51

Sir, I commend to you the spirit
Of Lucifer, who was most beautiful
And wore in that proud skull
Rebellion like a jewel exquisite;
I adjure you to meekly admit
That seething genius pre-punctual,

Foreword to all the historical:
I beg you to give him his meet.

Brightest of archangels and brightest
Of demons—proud, incomparable Lucifer!
I alone of all men remember
And praise that magnificent zest
That sent God frantic to abuse
And doom this First, pioneering Genius.

52

Come to a conference with me!
We will confer About,
Till you are in Doubt.
This is the first Circumstance.

Come to a conference with me!
We will confer About,
Till you reject Without.
This is the second Circumstance.

Come to a conference with me!
We will confer About,
Till you see God Turned About.
This is the Immortal Circumstance!

53

I unfell completely from
As I fell completely into:
The Act most pure.

Than purity more clear
And excelling it:
But here was purest trapezist.

With a brilliance of spirit
Agiler than mathematics
Preciser than God

I equated Life to Fire
In clearest ethics
And so—I am called Immoralist.

54

Now, if you will look in my brain
You will see not Because
But Cause—
The strict Rose whose clean
Light utters all my pain.
Dwelleth there my God
With a strict Rod
And a most luminous mien.

And He whippeth! lo how
He whippeth! O see
The rod's velocity
In utterest unmercy
Carve, inflict upon this brow
The majesty of its doomèd Now.

55

Myself solving myself—
Myself Eye and Seen,
Patient and Psychologue—
With only God between.

Standing proud, immutable!
Dark, impenetrable!
The Power that balanceth me
Pierceless, immovable!

Away, my Lord! Away!
Leave thou a path to see
This formidable clay!
Create graceful vacancy,

Resign this Regency!
Else bear the terrible hell
Of Creator swerved aside
By mortal's brave scalpel.

56

Imagination is Where God
Would have been born
    But for Heaven,—
Yet that it comprises more
But increases the stature of its door.

Because that it weds
Both Heaven and Hell
    And giveth Angel
Brother in Devil—it may not
Except by true gods be subjugate.

Even God, when He enters
Imagination's door—lo!
    He must bow—
It is such a Terrible Door
He enters with golden terror.

But Within—lo, behold
The Greatest Nativity—
    The Nativity
Of Everness—more immortal
Than His own Soul.

57

I was not young long: I met the soul early:
Who took me to God at once: and, seeing
God the Incomparable Sight, I knelt my body

Humbly: whereupon God saw the star upon
My brow: stooped to kiss it: O then the
Blinding radiance there! explosion of all

My earthness: sparks flying till I was all
Embers: long, long did God hold me: till
He arose and bade me to rise saying: Now

Go back. Now go back from where you came.
Go back: Understanding is yours now. Only
Beware: *beware!* since you and God have lovered.

58

My mouth is very quiet
Reverencing the luminance of my brain:
If words must find an outlet
They must work with jewelled pain.

They must cut a way immaculate
To leave the brain incorrupt:
They must repay their Debt
Like archangels undropt.

The miracle of a word is to my mouth
The miracle of God in my brain:
Archangels holding to His North and South,
His East and West by an inviolable chain.

An archangel upon my mouth
May blow his silver trumpet:
But he holds to his North or South,
Blows—and again is quiet.

59

From seeming to being is forever.
From birth
To forever.

Being's seeming is not ever.
Being
Will not seem.

Is, is sovereign, nor needs
Applause.
Is independent rose.

60

The way my ideas think me
Is the way I unthink God.
As in the name of heaven I make hell
That is the way the Lord says me.

And all is adventure and danger
And I roll Him off cliffs and mountains
But fast as I am to push Him off
Fast am I to reach Him below.

And it may be then His turn to push me off,
I wait breathless for that terrible second:
And if He push me not, I turn around in anger:
"O art thou the God I would have!"

Then He pushes me and I plunge down, down!
And when He comes to help me up
I put my arms around Him, saying, "Brother,
Brother." . . . This is the way we are.

61

Now let us announce me.
This is a very grave duty.
Let us announce me.
Announce me perfectly.

I am most of all, most.
The least of me is most.
God can see almost
The most He got to almost.

He was almost I
Until He could not die.
I was almost He
Until I learned to disagree.

62

Between one and one
Between integer and integer
Is itself's nothing
The abstract zero.

Between I and I
Between self and self
Is itself's everything
The abstract Hero

That self may equate to
Or keep ever as two.

63

To give you my permanent address
Will astound you
As myself have.
The days of no address
Or the days of interrogation
Are gone.
Have found.

Migration has escalade
Up or down
Or width here to there
But always a focus
An always-address.

Found.
Could have been Death
Had not Love supremed me.

Might have been less than
Death, or more.
But when God heard it
He abdicated grandly

And I was there without sound—
The Word.

64

Saw God dead but laughing.
Uttered the laugh for Him.
Heard my skull crack with doom
Tragedian laughing!

Peered into the cracked skull—
Saw the tragic monkhood

In the shape of God's deathhead
Laughter upon its mouth a jewel.

Jewel bright, O Jewel bright,
Laughter of the Lord.
Laughter with eternity immured
O laugh bright, laugh bright.

Then did the Lord laugh louder
I laughing for Him,
I from the heart's honeycomb
Feeding braver, braver,

Till all the universe was Laughter
But the Laughter of the Lord
O the Laughter of His Word
That could laugh only—after His murder.

65

Only birds, only mirrors
The unadulterated eye
Can see me. Their quick thought
Quickly congratulates

My braveries, my ardours,
My revolutionary sky,
My pledges, my truths unbought,
My axioms and postulates.

Congratulates without script
Being pure unenemies,
Unacademes and strict
Against falsities.

Degree without manuscript,
Degree without cease,

Over the purest conflict
The cleanest theologies.

66

Everybody is a who.
Everybody is a nude.
Not always I am you,
Sometimes I.
Sometimes not at all.

God too is a who,
God too is a nude.
But His is a story Of
Ours only a story when.
Sometimes not at all.

Our whos differ
As we have stories Of,
Or stories when,
Or of not at all.
Between these
Looms the Terrible Wall.

Sometimes not at all.

67

Since my Correspondence
With God
Dates all my luminance.
'Tis our Communions

Gives me pinions.
From Him
All my dazzling opinions—
Yet anonymous He

But for me! His Verity
Unworded,
His conclusions in bankruptcy
Without my Finality!

68

My most. My most. O my lost!
O my bright, my ineradicable ghost.
At whose bright coast God seeks
Shelter and is lost is lost. O
Coast of Brightness. O cause of
Grief. O rose of purest grief.
O thou in my breast so stark and
Holy-bright. O thou melancholy
Light. Me. Me. My own perfidy.
O my most my most. O the bright
The beautiful the terrible Accost.

69

Flew birds east where I was.
Flung back the sun to see.
Fled in terror of Divinity
Brothering his Judas.

Birds! birds! birds!
My immortality is such
That I must love overmuch.
Yet a terror of herds

Seizes me, such a terror
As no mirror of hell can divulge.
Then who must assuage?
Judas, Judas!—Aggregate Traitor.

70

So that it could be essence
The history of within:
This was the method
My soul made for sin—

Beneath the circumstance
Of sensual lust
The divinest God
Uprose from the sinful crust.

He had not known me
Without the senses' mystery!
Only the exactitude of sin
Had revealed Him within!

71

Or I myself in death
As I ascended—Death being more
Than philosophy. There was a Door
Made me hold my breath

And He was Outlined there.
Who? Who the Apparition?
Subject me to no explanation—
O but it was Flaming there!

The Outline of Fire
With velocity of Eternity!
But who? who?—Anonymity?
Most certainly not. Die—and aspire!

72

Then when He said no I knew yes.
There was no reason to say yes.
He said no.
But I knew yes.

I went ahead.
He said no, I knew yes.
I went ahead.
There was no reason not
I knew yes.

Knowing yes, going ahead, I knew no.
There was no reason not
He said no
I remembered He said so.

73

Nevermore to delay life
End the beginning
Devise the bravest perpendicular
To the squarest circle.

Assume the ending.
If He lies broken who broke Him?
Assume your innocence!

If you are broken who broke you?
Assume His innocence!

The perpendicular of heaven and death!
Now the wounded may rest.
If He—on your breast.

If you—on His breast.
Rest, rest.

74

Time the traveller
Bringeth us little specimens
We call experience:
But the great Essences

The things not specimens
These must be of our Own Blood!
A resident God
Our beautiful blood's miracle.

In our blood's laboratory
We have this Task to do,
The Distillation of the Dew
With passion of the Tormented.

Till prismed in the blood,
O luminous and glowing,
We see this royal God bowing
Our lovely Parentage acknowledging!

75

Often, the livingness of death
More is than the livingness of life:
Then is the face of death
Brillianter than the face of love.

Creatrix of the austere fire
Death has a sensuous skull:
Peerless, merciless Beauty rare!
She is the Rose Original.

She is the merciless beauty
Of Hierusalem, whose pleasaunce
Is despair—whose peerless piety
Seduced Jesus for the Tree.

76

Sir, there's a tower of fire in me
Binding me with terrible strength
The whole of my mortal length
And splitting brave the skull's empery
In a rush of dauntless energy
To reach the most luminous ether.
I am the mortal grounding of a tower
Imminent with immortality.

The reasons of my skull avail not
Against this rush of fire, and whether
I assent or not, I am the creature
Must uphold the merciless bigot—
But I am loyal to the earth though through my skull
Descend God the Burning Jewel, like my betraying angel.

77

Were death not so involved
(I mean not the flesh's death)
I should long have resolved
The tactics of her faith.

Her tissues move unmusketed,
Her soldiery is lean;
Their sandals are blanketed,
Yet they cut most keen.

Her soldiers are devout,
Their pulses are delicate;

They keep no route,
Nor argue to debate—

But in phalanx move as one,
A fleet of angels, satin-shod;
They kiss like angels, every one,
And poison like an inverted God.

78

Mostly are we mostless
And neverness is all we become.
The tiger is tigerless
The flame is flameless.

Dig up Time like a tiger
Dig up the beautiful grave
The grave is graveless
And God is Godless.

I saw myself reflected
In the great eye of the grave.
I saw God helpless
And headless there.

Until I put my head on Him.
Then He uprose superb.
He took the body of me
And crumpled me to immortality.

79

Futurity's equivalence to Now
Is incurable.
How far to see
Is my problem.

To divide futurity rightly.

First, God, if you can remember
He is not undiscriminative love.
Unmythed God.
I unchurched Him and charged
Him manfully.

God is Alive now.

Possibility of His death is remote
He having now my head.
God's old head I have given
To the crows.
His old eyes are pecked out
And dead!

Therefore I charge you, God,
To be careful of my head!

"I will be careful."

Be careful of my head!

80

Faithfullest, for I am infidel!
Lexicon—renew thy charge!
Defeated antonymity,
Conjugated marge!

Of Infidel—to disavow
Be his true symmetry—
To unknow—
His brave geometry—

Yet such my Infidelity
As by her pure artillery
—Firing, she but teaches Him
His Brightest Angelity!

81

In life I shone with so much death:
(For death is so very bright—
To see her splendid sight
Maketh to hold the breath).

With so much death I shone, I shone:
Many could not look at me
But thought such beauty savagery:
The lesser stooped to pick a stone.

And cast it at this Savage strange.
And cast it at my Light.
But none could dim my bright
That from Death was her pure exchange

For the heart I burnèd for her sake,
For the mind I brokèd for her sake.

82

O, the brightness of my dark!
Dark inwove of Light—
Where to grope is to see
That unconfrontable Instancy

Of my Lord God stretchèd stark,
Maniac without sight,

Upon the burning meridian
Of this ambitious brain.

Lo, thou espousèd there!
Lo, thou naked Rasputin!
Why wilt not arise and blare
Thy terrible chagrin

At this brain of thy make?
Why lieth trodden silent
When chagrin can slake?
"Because I am reverent."

83

How shines my dark-world
Upon the sun! and gives it
Light for the earth-world—
While I lie in darkest defeat,
In dark most terror-complete.

How shines the sun-world
Upon the earth-world! and feeds it
My brilliance terror-hurled—
The sun's immortal deceit,
Assumption of my immortal feat!

Be absolved, Sun, be absolved:
But only in the name of Love—
My dark-world God-revolved,
My dark-world you have pity of!

84

Progress from no or yes
Progress from life or death.

Progress from who
Or progress from not-who.

I progressed from Christ.
Christ progressed from me.
Whoever progresses from us
Progresses to secrecy.

Christ is my secret
I His secret!
I the Cross upon Him
He the Cross upon me.

I the Hand across His mouth
He the Hand across my mouth.
I the Word breaking His mouth
He the Word breaking my mouth.

85

The contraband of soul
Amongst mortality!
  We must hide it
In direst secrecy!

Lest it be known to all
And their fingers point
  "Judas!"—and fit
Us to the beams conjoint!

86

I betook me to the ways of Truth,
I burnished me for the field of death,
I tautened this fragile breath
So it could compass life with ruth—

I marshalled the beautiful skull
To look for the great undeath,
I found the necessary faith
In my heart that brave jewel.

So here was I, seeker and assaulter,
With Life to probe and prove:
In chastest ways only did I move
To find that great ultimate Center.
In this Diagram without fault
Lo, behold me—Center of the divine assault!

87

If: or: maybe.
These are the divisor words.
The Holy Ghost made these cruelties

In the image of His kindness.
These words divide justly.

To the honor of Love
The divisor words divide the heart
Purely. The cisions are clean.
The blades are keen.
The anguish has an immortal mien.

88

It is necessary to die livingly.
It is very necessary to do this.
I have every death of a life.
You can see it in my death.

Very well it is a commandment.
Go everyone to die livingly!

I am living with a command,
I command death very livingly.

It is necessary to do this.
Heart and brain must die livingly!
I have every life of a death.
You can see it in my life.

89

Now of two deaths
Life-death, Death-death
Look to the first:
The expiration by Thirst

The expiration within.
Now I died this way and
Created the vital death
Validing the final death.

Easily: for the dial was set in
Life: so Death ticked pure,
Timed in pulsing blood.
Now this is not death but God.

90

Within the city of my death
Comes Death melancholy,
For that he seeks to reap me
Who gave God His Head.

Yet if he touch me, ah! he
Slays but the body alone,
Still upon its Throne
Shall sit my Head.

Poor Death! who can no
More call me dead
Unless he kill my Head:
And that forever is upon

His Shoulders and He proud
To wear it, His diadem
From Life, the gem
He died for. So Death—*I live!*

91

By death only. Her revival of infinity
Declaimed silently. And this only.
My heart is there at the prophetic mouth.

Will you propel me fairly, Death?
Will you language me commensurately?
Meanwhile, I am Spanish, caballero.

In this ravishing world I am polite.
Tip my hat though inwardly I spit.
Because my heart is bitter at your

Prophetic mouth. My brain is gay.
My limbs are sensual. My heart only
Has the perils of immortality.

92

I told God to go away—
"For Thou art sick and can not
Bear man's beauty:
Then, do Thou away and not

Come back till Thy Eyes see well:
Be Thy Body robust,
Thy Heart clean to spell
The beauty of mortal lust.

Away then my Lord till Thou
Art purified! I myself
Will know Thee then, and seek Thee
In man's behalf.

But now Thou must away—
Thou must, lest Thou rot
Excessive in Adam's eye
And he . . . forgive Thee not."

93

For which I designed God perishable—
For I have designed man illustrious:
In whom He must seek hermitage
And break His austerity!

So have I made God perishable
Finite, lean and homeless:
Till His need brave Him to merge
With Adam's mortal beauty.

Let His eyes then be forever triste
In most agony of the Christ!
Until He learn this couplement
For His perfect Jerusalem.

Aye, I His poet make this Tryst
For I would have Him capsized!
That He arise in healment
Perfect and a Gem.

94

Christ adventuring in my mind.
Christ bedding, loving a woman.
Christ Progenitor.

And you sulking, slinging me slime
You denouncing, damning me
Because my Christ is beautiful!

Christ living, human in my mind.
Christ honest, laughing, singing,
Nude musical!

95

In the chamber of my philosophy
God is instructed.
God is all naked
For reception of my energy.

God is all naked.
I am all incandescent.
God must begin His ascent
To me the Created.

God is instructed
In the ways of humanity.
God must humanize divinity
To be perfected.

God is my elected.
Him have I chosen
To be berosen.
Him have I elected.

God is my miracle!
God is my Work!
Music from the stark,
Original, marble Syllable!

96

First add-subtract
Until Identity.
Then to counteract
Divide-multiply

Until Unity.
Both emprised,
This mortality
Achieveth Christ—

Both comprised,
This perfection
Is dissolution!
Immortalled Christ!

97

God fears the poems of
Such as I!
Who am neither blind
Nor sly:

For that though I praise Him
I accuse!
His inhuman Godhood
I refuse.

For that though I seek Him
I repel Him!

Repulsion so great
As to unnerve Him.

Dissolution of God
Is my end:
That His Nullity
I may forfend.

Dissolution of the
Spermless God:
To the Aristocracy
Of the Living Blood.

98

Are you waiting for God's Word
With so much patience?
Are you waiting and waiting
In clamor or silence?

Arise! Wait no more!
In the end is only one's own nakedness!
Though God himself cleave to thee
Alas! He is messageless.

All He can do is embrace thee:
His mind was long ago dead.
He cleaveth to thee so meek:
Be gentle, be gentle to this crazèd Head!

99

Now I will tell you the Future
Of God. The future of God is

Man. God aspired before and
Failed. Jesus was too much

God. Since God is moving
Towards Man, and Man is moving

Towards God—they must meet
Sometime. O but God is always

A Failure! That Time is the
End of the world. When God

And Man do meet—they will
Be so bitter they will not speak.

100

Imagine God a peacock—
Imagine Him crucified,—
Over Him the beauty
Of great peacock feathers.

The Cross of the Peacock
Must not be denied.
Here begins our duty
To say our peacock prayers.

O Lord of peacocks,
Behold Thy tribe below!
O Peacock God,
Hear our peacock prayers!

God as a Peacock
Can suffer no shock.
Nazarene as Narcissu,
Behold all mankind bowing to you!

101

With every word, with every thought
With every act,
Besmirched I God;
But He, to counteract

Came down to calm the cruel mouth
And kiss the rebel brow,
And said not a word,
Nor loud, nor low!

And kissed once more the rebel brow,
In Godhood's mystery.
But I, where God touched me,
O frantic! sought immediate cautery.

102

The wind shines,
    The sun blows:
The leaves dig,
    The roots unfold—

We are looking in the mirror
Of Narcissu!

The birds bloom,
    The flowers fly:
The bees sing,
    The birds sting!

We are looking in the mirror
Of Narcissu!

Who is very beautiful
Being Jesus,

Who is very sorrowful
By this mirror—

Seeing the image of man
Reflected there

(*O the wind shines,*
The sun blows:
The leaves dig,
The roots unfold)

O that very strange glass
O that very strange glass
Where the image of man
Is Judas.

103

Then we came unsinging
Because having looked at God
He was unrememberable!
There was nothing to say, He
Himself could not say the Word.

His priests, however, went on lying
They that never saw God.
But we who had seen Him were not able
To lie. Speechless we went our way
Muted in unmemory of the Lord.

104

Sphinx-mouthed Sage whose
Secret was uttered by
    The Crucifixion:
Accept the Lie
Of Mankind that
    Heard Thee not!

Who threw Thee a paper mourning-rose
At Thy Resurrection,
    Jubilant
In paper religion
As at a carnival
    's carousal—

Accept the Fact that Even Thou
Must bend before
    Humanity's
Dark uncancellable brow—
Eternal fountain-ore
    Of the Judas Kiss—

Accept Defeat! Accept Defeat!
Hope no more,
    O Deluded!
It is terribly writ
That for ever and ever
    Thou bleed!

105

I made myself to burn
Brightly to seek and learn
The unknowable temperature
Of God's Calenture.

My mind I pitched to
Direst fever, as few
Or none ever may know:
I reached that glow!

Fevered to the bright, grand
Temperature, lo! His princely hand
Smote the lance of my mind:
"Not by the mind, O Blind!"

106

God not looking, sudden
   I gripped His heart:
Cleft it in twain—division
   Swift and alert,

Cision by the deft hand,
   His Godhead's clue
Finally to unwand
   As the mind's long due.

Immortal tissue riven,
   Yet shrank I not;
But bent the mouth brazen
   To the bleeding cut.

Ah, His secret was not fair,
   O but so bitter!
My lips may not again fare
   On blood of Cavalier!

107

Inexplicacy of birth
Has given me God's eyes!
Miracle against earth
That my soul defies.

Ah, look into my eyes and see
God's very Potency!
See the Power and the Glow
The ultimate Yes or No

Tremble on the verge of
My human eyes: God's lens

Through which I see—all of love:
And die of His immortal suspense!

108

Silentness is not Silence.
He's silent in silence whose
Soul's geography is bare.

But silentness is deportment
Heroic, when the field is
Occupied. He's silent in

Silentness—whose God is there,
Or when God lies dying,
A finger to His lips. *Hush!*

109

Allow God's cowardice
A design—
Then it shines divine.
Bear Him no malice—

He will bloom the Word.
Though it come
The unforgettable Sum
At the tip of a sword.

110

Days of my youth
Call my amaze,

Held I so much Truth
In so young a Blaze.

How kept I all
Without faint from Heat?
Who signed my Scroll
To be without limit?

I know, I know!—
The Angel Jesu!
Right on my brow
In mortality's lieu.

111

When I mimic God,
And act His omnipotency—
   Lo, how grand
Is His courtesy!

How gallantly He watches,
Without least murmur
   Or demur,
Comprehending my fever.

But when God mimics me—
I stand in human rage
   Unable, unable
To watch the stage!

112

Equality? Our
Souls equal?
   As well say
Intersects are parallel.

Firmament of star
Heaven centrifugal
  These have a way
Distinct, unequivocal.

Elements, compounds
Of the Greater Rounds,
  These—equal
To the Decimal?

113

God is Love . . .
Priest's dixit!
Lie infinite
Of the Pulpit!

Making God
Indiscriminate,
In vain His
Son's novitiate.

Nay, God makes
Strictest choices.
His Ledger demands
Brightest Invoices!

114

I will bespeak the mordaunce
In God's heart. I threw the lance
That set it there. I know
Then the potency of the blow.
He moved not as I raised the
Lancèd hand. He stood a body
Whole of love. He commanded not

The hand's desistance. He cut
The figure of Loneness against
The sky. But my will was earnest!
I sent the lance and hurled him
Down. He fell on the rough rim
Of the earth. I helped him not
To rise. He arose and reviled not.
He walked to me but then I ran.
I am everyone called Man.

115

Death, corollary to Life
But only by Chronology.
Death, the supreme Theorem—
Life, the Corollary.

Whose antecedence—
Paradox divine—
Mathematicus Sublime
Created in inversed line.

A progression of wine
From fruit to poem.
Grape, the Corollary,
Wine, the Theorem.

116

A brilliance met me,
I was returning lifeward
Moving deathward. A brilliance
Like music not music

A brilliance like sun.
Do you not see it?

A brilliance majestic
Like an imperishable word.

For I was a poet and death
And brilliant as despair
And moving deathward
To see lifeward.

Brilliance and brilliance
Together coming! O brilliances
All exceeding! At last
Christ with Judas.

117

In contest for myself
I live and do;
And such my atomy
Not to contest self

Itself should detest.
The investment is small—
Only the mortal I,—
Yet expenditure can appall

And leave self aghast.
But never capital expel
If atomy bear
Blood of His bequeathèd Ghost.

118

Had I not this life decreed,
With a clarity passional,
Most self to deed
With strictest diagonal,

It had not chosen love
Nor distilled it,
Nor audited proof
So oblique and exquisite.

Not merited, not heard
The birth of that Debt,
Of that syllable The Word
Heard only in the ricochet.

119

Now, there dwelt in me
Great unwisdom, of great decorum;
Of evil pride,
And great beauty:

Marching me with splendor,
Moving men to homage, whom
Their eyes denied
Visibility of horror.

But I saw Criste at last
Who rent my mask to doom:
Lo, how these men cried
And turned me Outcast!

120

Now that now
You are truer old
Time to learn to bow
Time to learn to hold

Self in homage.
Time to know to burn

With purer rage
Time to know to scorn

Unself in any place
In any when, in any with.
Time to unveil the face
Of the unknown pith:

Time to claim its grace
Time to confront this Face.

121

Does a mirror forget?
I believe it does not.
I believe a mirror will not forget
If you come to it superb.

Clear gaze of mirrors
Towards the gaze of God:
As the waters of Galilee
Upholding the superb Feet.

122

A wall is History.
I say, Illuminate this
To see Who hang there.
Their Instantness never will cease.

Not to see is not to unsee them.
The not-seer cannot unmake.
Sweet, murdered stars
Upon the solid black stake

Drift history immortalward.
Extension of the Wall

Is due in every Now.
Otherwise the Fire will fall.

123

A true wrath requires reason.
A way of Truth is wrath.
Truth having no season
Truth may choose time and path.

The time of wrath is pure
When Truth is upward.
And path is Signature
Upon the chosen Guard.

Evilness in such is never.
He climates the Absolute.
This lightning fever
Requires imperial salute.

124

The shadow of a great man
Is always Christ.
Under the raiment
Looms the inevitability life-sized.

And who must speak
If not this Shadow?
Though it counterspeak the law
It need not go on tiptoe

Being the Christ Shadow:
Purity Intangible,
With death's agility
To be uncrucifiable.

125

Always I did want more God
Than life could yield,
More God than God could give.

I betook me to His Rood,
Made it my chosen Field,
That I might truly live.

I bled in direst blood
And by Him twi-distilled,
Yet eluded He me as through a sieve.

Till He loosed again His Blood,
And over my soul it ruby-spilled,
And wove it into lovely mercy's Hive.

126

Always and always the amaranth astir
Ages and ages assailing man the fair
Assuaging now afflicting now man the alone
Asking answers atop and across the bone.

Aliment of another air another star
Amator of all the alive and of attar
Amorous and adored, O altar of lovers fair
Assail now the less amorous and less fair.

Adam and all Adam's young address and arrest
Afflict these with the music-auroral breast
Atone at last for the agony of Jesus most fair
Always and always teach His ascension rare.

127

Greatly imagine me, my God,
As greatly I imagine you: You will see
That my image is a load
You can most proudly bear:
My movements in you shall stir
Manly immortality.

Make me your living Forehead!
'Grave me beyond perishment as I
'Grave you so that you always lead.
As you are my spirit's end,
Make me your spirit's own! Bend
O bend to my urgency.

Be the Great Imaginer. Imagine me
Yourself tri-solved: O believe in Mortality.

A NOTE ON *REVERSED CONSONANCE*

The author is pleased to introduce in this book a new method of rhyming, a method which has never been used in the history of English poetry, nor in any poetry. This method is used in poems 1, 4, 9, 12, 16, 45, and 47.

The principle involved is that of *reversed* consonance. The last sounded consonants of the last syllable, or the last principal consonants of a word, are reversed for the corresponding rhyme. Thus, a rhyme for *near* would be *run*; or *rain, green, reign*. For *light—tell, tall, tale, steal*, etc.

In the case of a word where no consonant follows the last vowel, as in

Leaned in my eyes and loved me

the corresponding rhyme is found by considering the last sounded consonant of the preceding word: thus, a corresponding rhyme, in this case, would be

It to a dazzeling diamond made.

Other possible rhymes for this case, then, could be *maid, mood,* etc.

To illustrate with a full poem, showing each consonantal reversion, rhyme by rhyme, I quote poem 1. The rhyme scheme is a-b, a-b:

It is what I never *said*,	(a)
What I'll always si*ng*—	(b)
It's not found in *days*,	(a)
It's what always begi*ns*	(b)
In half dark, in half *light*.	(c)
It's shining so cur*ved*	(d)

Yet rises so tall and *te*lls (c)
Where the first flower *dov*e (d)
When God's hands lost *lov*e. (e)
It's a great word without sou*nd* (f)
Without echo to re*veal* (e)
Where fragrance went *down*! (f)
O, but it's all of it *the*re (g)
Above my poems a W*reath*. (g)

That this new method of rhyming can be used successfully, the author demonstrates in the poems he has mentioned. In the author's belief, this new rhyme method is subtler and stricter, and less obtrusive on the ear, than ordinary consonance.

JGV

from *VOLUME TWO*
(1949)

A NOTE ON THE COMMAS

The reader of the following poems may be perplexed and puzzled at my use of the comma: it is a new, special and *poetic* use to which I have put it. The commas appear in the poems *functionally*, and thus not for eccentricity; and they are there also *poetically*, that is to say, not in their prose function. These poems were conceived *with* commas, as "comma poems," in which the commas are an integral and essential part of the medium: regulating the poem's verbal density and time movement: enabling each word to attain a fuller tonal value, and the line movement to become more measured. The method may be compared to Seurat's architectonic and measured pointillism—where the points of color *are* themselves the medium of expression, and therefore functional and valid, as medium of art and as medium of personality. Only the uninitiate would complain that Seurat should have painted in strokes.

Regarding the time movement effected by the commas—a pause ensues after each comma, but a pause not as long as that commanded by its prose use: for this reason the usual space after the comma is omitted. The result is a lineal pace of quiet dignity and movement.

I realize of course that this new poetic employment of the comma is an innovation which may disconcert some readers: for them I can only say that they can *still* read the poems by ignoring the commas if they find these in the way; personally I find that they even add visual distinction. With the more poetically and texturally sensitive reader, I believe that he will see with me the essentiality of the commas: the best test, which I have myself employed, is to copy out a poem *omitting* the commas and then to read this text comparatively with the comma'ed version: the loss is distinctly and immediately cognizable.* Therein lies the justification for this—true enough—strange innovation.

JGV

---

*To satisfy the reader on this point, I have included in the book two poems in two versions each: with and without the commas. The reader may now do his own judging. See poems 130 and 134. In the tampered versions (without the commas) the lines run faster and the effect of the poem is flat.

DIVINE POEMS

128

The,bright,Centipede,
Begins,his,stampede!
O,celestial,Engine,from,
What,celestial,province!
His,spiritual,might,
Golding,the,night—
His,spiritual,eyes,
Foretelling,my,Size;
His,spiritual,feet,
Stamping,in,heat,
The,radium,brain,
To,Spiritual,Imagination.

129

Purely—
In,two,ways:
In,two,ways,
Purely.

In,most,action:
Creative,death.
In,most,unaction:
Creative,life.

Sternly—
In,creator's,ways:
Life,and,death,
Dividing,a,single,face.

130

Much,beauty,is,less,than,the,face,of,
My,dark,hero. His,under,is,pure,
Lightning. His,under,is,the,socket,

Of,the,sun. Not,Christ,the,Fox,not,
Christ,the,Lord,His,beauty,is,too,
Sly,too,meek. But,Christ,Oppositor,

Christ,Foeman: The,true,dark,Hero.
He,with,the,three-eyèd,thunders,he,
With,the,rigorous,terrors: this,

Man's,under,is,pure,lightning. This,
Man's,under,is,the,socket,of,the,
Sun. After,pure,eyes,have,peeled,

Off,skin,who,can,gaze,unburned? Who,
Can,stand,unbowed? Well,be,perceived,
And,well,perceive. Receive,be,received.

(130)

Much beauty is less than the face of
My dark hero. His under is pure
Lightning. His under is the socket

Of the sun. Not Christ the Fox, not
Christ the Lord, His beauty is too
Sly, too meek. But Christ Oppositor,

Christ Foeman: The true dark Hero.
He with the three-eyèd thunders, he
With the rigorous terrors: this

Man's under is pure lightning. This
Man's under is the socket of the
Sun. After pure eyes have peeled

Off skin, who can gaze unburned? Who
Can stand unbowed? Well be perceived
And well perceive. Receive, be received.

131

No; I,will,not,speak,softly—
I,am,Thy,lover,Lord!
So,I,meet,Thee,with,the,sword,
Of,my,utter,Love.

And,dare,Thee,to,wreck,me,
With,my,own,sword,
If,my,Love,is,not,heard—
Do,Thou,move,

This,hand,me-wards,
O,shatter,me,to,shards,
If,Thou,canst,not,bear,
This,Cataract,in,the,air.

132

Before,one,becomes,One,
The,labor,is,prodigious.
The,labor,of,un-oneing,

To,become,a,One!
The,precision,of,un-oneing,
The,procedure,of,dissembling,

Is,the,process,of,expiation,
For,the,sin,of,Nothing.
This,Absurdity,is,Unification.

133

The,Reason,Why—
Is,not,Because:
But,is,a,farther,coast,
A,deeper,Cause,
Often,lost.

Yet,though,it,
Were,not,lost,
It,is,of,Cost,irredeem-
able,by,Because—
Because,is,

Dead: a,dead,
Hand,clasping,
The,Cause! I,burned,all,
Becauses,till,
Sternly,I,

Uprose: A,Pure,
And,this,was,
Rebellion: God,at,last,
On,His,buckling,
Stallion!

134

When,I,was,no,bigger,than,a,huge,
Star,in,my,self,I,began,to,write,
My,
Theology,
Of,rose,and,

Tiger: till,I,burned,with,their,
Pure,and,Rage. Then,was,I,Wrath-
Ful,
And,most,
Gentle: most,

Dark,and,yet,most,Lit: in,me,an,
Eye,there,grew: springing,Vision,
Its,
Gold,and,
Its,wars. Then,

I,knew,the,Lord,was,not,my,Creator!
—Not,He,the,Unbegotten—but,I,saw,
The,
Creator,
Was,I—and,

I,began,to,Die,and,I,began,to,Grow.

(134)

When I was no bigger than a huge
Star, in my self I began to write
My
Theology
Of rose and

Tiger: till I burned with their
Pure and Rage. Then was I Wrath-
Ful
And most
Gentle: most

Dark and yet most Lit: in me an
Eye there grew: springing Vision,
Its
Gold and
Its wars. Then

I knew the Lord was not my Creator!
—Not He, the Unbegotten—but I saw
The
Creator
Was I—and

I began to Die, and I began to Grow.

135

Oh,yes,I,am,looking,for,
Since,when,I,last.
The,very,face,is,past,

But,unaccountably,is,Future:
My,discovery,having,been,intact,
Not,breaking,into,fact.

The,witness,was,I,
Who,discovered,but,was,not,there!
Absence,thus,insurer,

Of,discovery,not,getting,away:
Discovery,made,acuter,
By,discoverer,not,there!

Had,discovery,come,with,presence,
Future,were,past,
Dead,in,a,cast—

But,this,discovery,has,durance—
Discoverer,not,there,
Giving,it,Fever.

The,witness,exists,
And,swears,to,the,Discovery!
Swears,to,its,Verity:

I,witness,swear,It,Is:
Myself,as,Absence,discoverer.
Myself,as,Presence,searcher.

136

My,whoseness,is,to,me,what,I,
Am,to,the,Holy,
Unghost—
It,moveth,me,
As,it,

Progresses,me,to,unnight,noon,
Day. Project,
Me,Unghost!
Project,me,
Elect,

Me,to,thy,knighthood,to,that,
Stern,height.
Knight,and,
Unnight,
Me. In,

Strictest,supervision,knit,me:
To,the,Gibralt,
Rock: to,the,
Radium,rock,
Of,I.

To,the,Gibralt,rock: to,the,
Radium,rock,of,
I. O,halt,
And,halter,
Me. Lead,

And,perish,me! Erect,me,to,where,
   All,eyesights,
       Break—
Let,all,eye-
       Sights,break!

137

The,soul,swarms,with,angels,
If,Soul,but,knew,it.
I,heard,an,angel,once,
Declaim,within,the,Orbit:

"Behold,us,thy,good,habitants—
Present,all,but,Kingless.
Arise,then,and,steer,us,
By,thy,Compass',grace!"

Ah,but,needle,would,not,move!
Compass,would,not,stir.
Sleep,was,so,velvet,
Soul,refused,to,be,Heir.

138

At,the,in,of,me,
More,real,than,unreality—
There,greens,an,infinity,

Ripens,and,does,not,fall:
Fruit,of,very-whole,
My,saint,my,prodigal.

Unbody,and,end,only—
Vision,and,end,only—
More,ill,more,beautiful,

More,still,more,musical,
Than,death,and,rose,in,love,
Than,rose,and,death,in,love.

139

By,His,eyes,felt,my,eyes—
By,His,ears,heard,my,say—
And,this,great,burning,me,
Rejecting,His,image.

Comparable,Lord,be,made.
Comparable,Lord,seek,doom:
Arise,incomparable,Human,
Arise,renewèd,Glow,and,Name.

Come,to,my,hands: *Be,molded.*
Descend,perfectable,Seed!
Break,in,my,hands,and,wake,
Perfect,in,need,and,love.

140

As,much,as,I,perceive,the,Future,
Lo: the,Future,perceives,me:
A,Mutuality,of,Eyes.

Untanglement,beyond,possibility—
Too,knit,too,knit,together,we!
None,can,effect,suture.

Not,I,if,I,wished: though,I,worked,
Though,I,broke,all,my,life:
Long,Ago,these,Futures,were,Weld:

Architecture,most,pure,most,splendid:
God,Pyramidal,Darkness—
And,I—Fire! climbing,it,climbing,it.

141

My,bright,Lion,coming,down.
Down,Jacob's,ladder,he,—
My,bright,Lion,coming,down!

Whatever,in,you,glows—
Whatever,in,you,can,praise—
(Laurel,fruit,or,stone)

To,my,bright,Lion,cast,it,now!
Look—in,his,mouth,
O,look—in,that,clean,mouth,

How,bravely,carries,he,
God,the,Dark,Corpse!
Out,of,Shining,Heaven,at,last.

142

In,my,undream,of,death,
I,unspoke,the,Word.
Since,nobody,had,dared,
With,my,own,breath,
I,broke,the,cord!

Dead,was,the,Word. Hurled,
To,its,tomb. Dead,
With,the,dead!
Alas,around,it,curled,
Behold: God,with,a,broken,head.

143

Clean,like,iodoform,between,the,tall,
Letters,of,*Death*,I,see,Life. This,
To,me,is,immortal,weather,immortal,

Spelling: The,elegant,interweaver,I,
Call,Hero. Beautiful,as,a,child,eating,
Raw,carrot: whole,as,a,child's,eyes,

Gazing,at,you: Death,builds,her,heroes,
Intensely,clean,Death,builds,her,heroes,
Intensely,whole. A,man,and,Death,indeed,

That,Life,may,speak: a,man,and,Death,
In,league,that,Life,may,flower: clean,
Athletic,mathematic,dancer: and,present-

Tensing,all,his,future: poises,dances,
Every,everywhere,he,go: Christ,upon,a,
Ball: Saltimbanque,perpetual,in,beauty.

144

I,was,old,very,young: I,was,all,
Mirrors: I,was,all,
Over,and,under,beside,and,around,

Inspecting,me. I,found,God's,
Unbearable,beauty!
I,found,His,thoughts,in,my,mind,

His,skull,in,my,hand! . . .
I,could,not,lay,
God's,skull,aside. I,preferred,suicide.

145

More,miracled,and,
Gazing,from,new,light-
Nings: from,blázerock,stérnrock,
I: journeyer,yet,I,go:
My,

Jacob,warlock,seek.
Footed,on,lightning,
Hobnail,in,fire: spy,from,my,Darien,
That,Who,that,When.
Whence,

I,derive: whence,is,
My,eye,anarch,and,love.
Then,come,Thou,must,O,Killer,Christ!
O,Killer,Christ,Thy,
Forepaw,

Sweet: in,dazelock,
Meet,my,Living,Arm:
Wrest,for,the,prize,of,Who,is,Who.
Well,Thee,I'll,lock!
Thy,

Rigid,blood,factor,
Thaw,Phosphor,to,Fire:
That,if,Thou,arise,Antarctic,Christ,
Yet,art,Thou,Glown,
To,

Heaving,Light. If,*I*,
Arise: Thou'rt,knelled,
Kneeled,to,O,succoured,from,marble,
Life: by,cavalier,Prometheus,
Love.

146

How,high,is,low,
If,it,resembles,high,
Yet,not,grows?

As,far,as,falsity,only,
Not,less,not,higher,
Not,reaches,Truth's,door,
Expires,as,it,aspires.

How,far,is,glass?
As,far,only,as,not,broken,
Not,more,not,less,
Than,this,single,address.

How,far,then,I,from,you?
As,far,only,as,I,
As,far,only,as,your,unbroken,glass,
Mirrors,serenely,the,broken,mouth,
Of,my,unbroken,unbreakable,mind.

147

How,young,art,thou?
As,young,as,after.
What,mean,after?
What,comes,before,
The,death,of,the,Brow.

I,met,a,seer,Thrice:
The,Father,the,Son,
The,Ghost. He,won,
From,me,the,price,
Of,Falsity's,overthrow.

And,that,was,Easter.
And,that,was,wonder.
And,that,was,fairer,
Than,bay-leaf,crown.
This,is,the,youngth,of,my,Brow.

148

The,baby,that,grows,up,from,old,age,
Will,have,youth,to,face:
A,startling,time.
A,difficult,time.

Having,been,real,
Reality,marches,to,sterner,reality:
A,not,possible,with,
The,baby,that,grows,up,from,youth.

A,devilish,time!
A,difficult,time!
When,Who,climbs,upward,
He,will,find,his,Face.

Not,so,the,youth,from,youth.
He,carries,a,faceless,face,
The,proud,imprint,
Of,his,general,race.

But,beware,of,the,baby,
Sprung,of,his,old,age!
His,Face,is,Terrible:
He,fronts,and,signifies,It.

149

Purity . . . before,I,
   Stepped,to,the,Door,and,

At,the,Door—
And,as,I,passed,
Out,the,Door . . .

Line,orbit,locus:
Peril,deed,and,map,of,
Blaze! Peril,
Of,immediate,
Hunter: daze,

Whirl,of,supreme,
Migrator: pull,of,his,
Gravite,anchor!
Fact,act,of,me,
To,me: Knitter:

Cleaver,of,me,Intact.

150

Today,the,spirituality,of,the,devil,
Challenges,the,deviltry,of,God.
Less,must,not,be,said;
More,can,not,be,said;
The,less,the,more,
The,devil's,spirituality,is,secure.

Religion,blows,no,wind,over.
God,has,learned,enough,deviltry,
To,be,the,devil,proper!
His,deviltry,also,is,secure.

The,trick,called,Eternity,
Will,judge,the,winner:
Today,is,too,late;
Tomorrow,is,too,soon;
Yesterday,is,too,past.

Long,ago,when,it,is,eternity,
Is,the,time,to,see.
This,waiting,is,finality!

151

What,is,defeat?
   Broken,victory.
Darkest,sanctuary,
But,solider,far,
   Than,the,triumphal,star.

Seek,then,no,argument,
   If,victory,is,served,
So,broken! Be,it,observed,
How,Life,is,compacter,
   By,this,glittering,disaster!

152

Came,I,then,upon,Lightning,as,still-life—
   Chemic,dancer,yet,panther,static:
      Whence,I,did,resolve—
"Thus,let,me,be. This,shall,be,I."

And,made,myself,utter-still,edged,as,knife:
   Loomed,great-electric,
      Above,my,Love:
Lo,He was,God: He,*dared!* I,flashed,and,
   He,did,die.

153

Somewhat,there,is,somewhere,
Where,is,somehow,somewho:

Where,thereward,to,go,is,
Himward,to,feel,believe,know.

Was,there,ever,such. Answer:
Yes. Ever,there,is,he. Yes.
Was,there,ever,when. Answer:
Yes. Ever,when. Even,now?
Answer: Even,now. Even,you?
Yes,and,even,I. And,even,

Even,the,yet,unborn.
Even,yet,those,not,yet,dead.
Question: What,Do,They?
Answer: They,finely,firmly,Love.

154

In,not,getting,there,is,perfect,Arrival.
Success,is,too,much,defeat!
The,laureateship,is,the,Way,as,Rival,
To,the,defeatless,Feet.

Jesus,never,got,there: He,arrived,
Perfectly. The,obstructive,Cross,
Uprose,as,Rival,and,contrived,
To,laurel,the,defeatless,Ghost.

155

To,be,central,or,God-I,
Came,Jesus,cross-high.
Unstrange,at,all,
Everybody's,clock,

Ticks,death's,weather.
To,commemorate,which,
Tombs,laud,the,last,page.

God-I,natheless,
Autobiographize,complete,
Central,on,the,first,page.

156

Jewels,do,not,glow,
For,external,eye,
These,design,purest,ray,
For,self,joy.

So,do,men,
Of,immortal,mien:
These,perform,
For,the,internal,firm.

Jewels,and,sun,
Self-beauty,scan:
Vanital,sin,
To,create,Ethical,Son.

157

Does,Death,revise?
No; he,merely,*reviews*.
Revisal,is,correction—
Review: Accepted,Circumstance.

Death,defies,
Any,Last,Excuse.
His,is,not,creation—
Your,Status,stands.

158

A,living,giant,all,in,little,pieces,
Out,of,death's,kingdom,into,shine—

My,dark,hero,out,of,death's,answers,
My,deep,hero,out,of,death's,mirrors:
My,living,brilliant,my,living,garnet.

He,dazzles,me,with,all,death's,emeralds!
He,death's,scholar,victor,flower:
All,death's,treasuries,all,death's,manuscripts,
All,death's,jewels,from,all,her,lives,
Locked,in,a,look,of,his,eyes—

He,seizeth,me,he,sizeth,me,he,driveth,me,
Out,of,my,kingdom,into,shine—
He,seizeth,me,he,driveth,me,he,raceth,me,
To,the,wild,and,gold,direction,
To,the,great,and,gold,destruction—

He,grazes,me,he,raceth,me,he,dazeth,me,
To,the,great,and,gold,answers,
To,the,bright,and,final,answers:
He,holdeth,me,he,goldeth,me,he,foldeth,me,
To,Living,Primogenite,Verb-living,Garnet.

159

What,is,equal,to,
Is,equal,to,

But,not,it.
Equality,is,

Achieved,relation,
But,the,equation,

Is,not,Identity.
Identity,is,

Solitary,Unit.

160

Crisp,is,God's,anger—
It,cracks,with,Tenderness.
He,is,so,much,Sun,
He,must,in,the,end,caress.

I,caused,His,anger,once,—
He,smote,the,dark,into,me,fierce!
But,then,it,broke,it,broke—
He,placed,me,again,amongst,His,peers!

161

There,are,three,Gentlemen—
   Each,has,no,name:
   No,one,says,mine:
   But,each,is,Who.

Have,three,shadows,three:
   One,source,one,wrath:
   Designed,each,to,betray,
   Each,of,the,other,Two.

They,He,the,Three,Gentlemen:
   The,Trisynonym!
   No,one,says,mine—
   Though,all,Life,they,draw.

162

As,Eternity,rests,poised,
On,Time's,reflection: so,doth,
   Definition,rest,
   On,Truth's,

Indefinition. "Was,Christ,
God?" The,truth,is,in,the,
   Surmise. Highest,
   Terms,move,

In,the,indirection,of,great,
Love . . . as,in,the,history,
   Of,night:
   Compassless,

And,without,sound: moves,
Most,visibly: the,majesty,
   Mystery,and,
   Purity,of,Light.

163

All,the,time,living,
Because,all,the,time,dying—
   Janushood:
   Double-burning.

When,Janus,is,wholly,burnt,
Having,paid,the,Tax,
   Behold,faceless,
   The,cleaner,wax.

164

The,hands,on,the,piano,are,armless.
No,one,is,at,the,piano.
The,hands,begin,and,end,there.

These,no-one's,hands,are,there:
Crystal,and,clear,upon,the,keys.
Playing,what,they,play.

Playing,what,they,are.
Playing,the,sound,of,Identity.
Yet,how,absurd,how,absurd,how,absurd!

165

Description of a Girl

Very,well,seen,by,the,lover,
    If,at,all. Or,her,mirror,or,
    Herself,in,the,bathing.
Who,can,describe,her,if,not,
    Her,lover: who,thinks,Shall,I,
    Really,mount,her,Shall,I,

Really,part,her,she,my,love?
    Describe,her,to,me. Describe,
    Her,to,me,young,lover!
Or,thou,mirror,which,says,I,
    Am,herself,yet,not,her,I,am,
    Herself,in,crystal,

Mathematics. Describe,her,to,
    Me. Or,herself,in,the,bath,
    Saying,My,lover,should,
Have,all,these,How,I,ache,to,
    Give,him,all,these,Come,have,
    All,these. Describe,her,to,me.

166

And,tell,of,the,corners,of,love,
    How,many,where! do,it,for,
    The,young,lovers. Tell,

Of,the,corners,of,love: where,where,
    How,many. Do,it,for,the,
    Young,lovers,who,are,not,

So,sure. They,must,know,for,to,love,
    Well. So,do,tell. Do,tell!
      "Then,listen,young,lovers,

"Love's,corners,be,but,two,but,
    Two,only,two. Love's,corners,
    Be,but,two,but,they,will,

"Do. But,two,but,all,for,you. One,
    Corner,the,lover's,it's,there,
    You,can,tell. One,corner,

"Hers,it's,there,you,can,tell. And,
    This,is,all,for,to,tell,
    Now . . . to,love,well!"

167

My,first,war,was,ten,
As,twelve,tall,waves—
I,combat,quester,the,sun,
My,eyes: I,dug,my,graves,
In,the,sun's,deep,eyes.

My,next,war,was,seven,
As,twelve,tall,sails—
I,combat,quester,the,moon,
My,eyes: I,dug,my,graves,
In,the,moon's,green,eyes.

My,third,war,was,five,
As,twelve,tall,gales—
I,combat,quester,the,fire,
My,eyes: I,dug,my,graves,
In,the,fire's,long,eyes.

My,fourth,war,was,three,
As,twelve,tall,Thieves—

I,combat,quester,the,truth,
My,eyes: I,dug,my,graves,
In,the,truth's,blind,eyes.

My,last,war,was,One,
As,twelve,tall,Christs—
I,combat,weary,with,death,
My,eyes: I,dug,my,Grave,
In,love's,true,eyes.

168

The,clock,was,not,a,clock,
Not,any,more,
It,was,a,watch.

The,watch,was,not,a,watch,
Not,any,more,
It,was,a,clock.

Both,said,Tick-tock,
Not,any,more,
They,said,Tock-tick.

Possibly,because,
Or,because,possibly,
Or,possibly,both.

Or,because,impossibly,
There,are,no,laws,
To,time,a,ghost.

169

Parthenogenesis of Genius

May,spring,from,*Un*-,
Light,and,lightning-like!
And,break,the,genetic,economy,

Springing,the,I-Absolute,
In,a,time-land,of,decimals:
Immaculate,conception,

Beyond,physiology—
Too,swift,for,prophecy,
Too,slow,for,tabloid,history.

Too,dim,too,near!
Too,far,too,bright!
The,Protagonist,of,the,age,

Mirrored,only,in,mirage.

170

With,on,my,pencil,the,youngest,flower,
My,darkest,grief,writes,down,its,light:
My,heart,is,slimmed,to,the,seven,arrows,
That,will,build,me,the,Lord's,peristyle.

This,depth,O,now,my,grief,will,climb,
And,reach,for,death's,deepest,bird!
Which,shall,prove,nor,male,nor,female,
But,it,of,the,burning,rose,in,the,rib.

God,will,ask,then,the,time,for,certain,
But,I,will,answer,with,never,a,word:
Till,He,cast,upon,me,His,burning,net,

And,entangle,me,in,its,burning,door!

Then,will,I,answer: *The,time,is,love.*
And,lo,He,will,pluck,my,two,eyes,out!
But,I'll,out,of,my,net,arise,and,veil,
God's,deed,from,all,of,Love's,principalities.

171

I,skirted,all,round,Heaven,
There,was,not,a,nook,of,dark,
Not,a,place,to,lay,the,head,on,
For,a,repose,of,sleep—

Save,within,the,hand,of,God,
Where,the,wounds,still,tell,
But,I,was,so,terribly,afraid,
Such,sleep,have,no,parallel!

Too,deep,too,deep,
Too,royal,a,dark—
Such,a,royal,landscape,
For,my,head,to,park!

172

Because,thy,smile,is,primavera,
A,nude,Botticelli: therefore,

Do,thou,smile,at,me. Because,
Thy,neck,is,proud,as,honey,

Dream,of,Modigliani: therefore,
Do,thou,come,queen,to,me.

And,because,thy,feet,are,small,
Though,I,bid,thee,run,to,me,

Do,thou,not,come,at,all,
But,let,me,run,quick,to,thee!

173

I,it,was,that,saw,
God,dancing,on,phosphorescent,toes,
Among,the,strawberries.

It,could,have,been,moonlight,or,
Daylight—or,no,light,at,all.
His,feet,cast,light,on,all.

On,phosphorescent,feet,
On,phosphorescent,feet,He,danced,
And,His,eyes,were,closed:

He,made,the,strawberries,tremble!
Yet,He,hurt,not,the,littlest,one,
But,gave,them,ripeness,all.

174

My,signature,is,that,part,of,me,
    Whose,terrible,agility,
Eludes,me,

As,essence,of,saint,
    Eludes,painter's,paint.
Such,restraint,

Equals,what,I,know,not.
    God,is,mystery-begot.
He,signatures,not.

175

Elegy for the Airplane

At,last,the,automobile,flew.
At,last,Icaros.
At,last,too,much.
At,last,too,fast.
At,last,the,present.

Flying,is,air-swimming.
Flying,is,bird-seeming.
Flying,is,death-daring.
At,last,meaning.
At,last,weaning.
At,last,morning.

Morning,is,evening,dead.
Mourning,is,for,the,dead.
Moving,is,for,the,head.
At,last,'tis,said.
At,last,we,were.
At,last,we,war.
At,last,we,fall.
At,last,we,all.
Alas,we,all.

APHORISMS, I

1

Count,7.
But,count,7 . . .
6,5,4,3,2,1.

2

An,Epigram,
Is,an,epic,Weight,

Concealed,
In,a,gram's,Space.

3

I,stood,Very,Still:
Sending,me,Orders.

4

Eternity,
Functions,without,motor.

5

There,is,a,bridegroom,
Of,no,lust—
Alas,alas,his,glory,is,
Spiritual,dust.

6

A,genius,is,he,
That,can,make,
Portable,pyramids.

7

There's,one,there's,two,
There's,three,of,Him.
Why,that's

Triplicity!

8

The,pages,of,a,mirror,
Are,translucent.

9

Gravitation's,more,
Than,Newton's,Law—
It's,the,pull,
Of,the,Grave.

10

"The,purpose,of,a,match?"
"To,start,a,fire,with."
No.
"To,store,up,fire,
And,to,keep,it,cool."

11

In,consummate,fatherhood,
To,count,not,heads,
But,fire.

12

We,find,what,we,do,not,find—
God,gives,with,His,hands,behind.

13

All,his,reasons,are,in,blue.
Therefore,all,his,reasons,
Are,in,gold.

14

A,diamond,intellect,
Believes,in,Light.

15

Extricate,
Extricate,God,
From,out,Creation's,terrible,net!

16

Education's,only,the,Envelope—
Give,me,the,Letter.

17

Foretell,not-love,by,stone.

18

Mathematician,excell,us,
Take,a,census,
Of,the,canaries,in,the,sun.

19

To,speak,of,the,interior,of,light,
Requires,speaker,broken,by,light.

20

What,is,told,in,diamond,
Is,not,glass—
It,has,more,than,
Planetary,elegance.

21

Precipices,and,peaks!
My,proud,geography.

22

There,are,three,windows,in,the,air!
So,that,the,Trinity,dividing,
May,Each,look,at,me.

23

The,descent,to,heaven,
Involves,the,tower,to,hell.
A,hell-sent,heaven,
Is,as,well,as,a,
Heaven-sent,hell.

Or,despair.

24

Only,the,hero,may,take,
A,snapshot,of,God.

And,then,it,would,be,
A,self-portrait.

25

The,Word. *Backing. Reversing!*

26

To,hold,the,breath,
Like,a,first-night's,bride—

Is,the,sense,of,jewels,
Must,exist,in,a,poem.

27

Mortality—my,precarious,Zone.
Complexity's,simplicity,
But,simplicity's,maze.

28

God,is,like,scissors,
Always,a,pair,
He,there,me,here.

29

Suspense—
The,fire,that,creates,Alaska.

30

A,bird,as,chrysanthemum,
Can,not,astonish,a,connoisseur:
Bird,will,unhide,from,flower.

31

Twin,me!

32

A,man,with,a,rose,for,his,mind,
And,a,rose,for,his,eyes—
What,has,death,to,do,with,him?

33

My,tongue,unBabeled,
Confuses,Babel,minds.

34

To,see,Trinity,in,minisculo.

35

Raise,the,angle,of,the,eye,
But,bend,
The,eye's,Knee!

36

A,hero,is,he,
That,can,write,
Letters,from,death.

37

A,promise,is,a,lavish,thing.
A,lavish,notness,outspread:
Phantom,lovers,upon,a,bed—
Or,realest,lovers,upon,a,phantom,bed.

38

This,little,cat,
Says,nine,thank-you's.

39

Death,faces,west,but,
I,face,east,and,
Count,always,seven.

40

To,be,broken,wholed:
What,a,process,to,speak,of,
By,so,simple,a,name,as,Love.

41

In,heaven,lies,recumbent,
God,
Religion's,ideal,corpse.

42

Poetry—
The,fight,for,insight.

43

With,simple,hands—
Like,the,first,hands,of,Adam,
Discovering,Eve.

44

The,soul,alone,
Has,copyright,on,God.

45

A,bee,flying,to,the,end,of,the,world,
To,find,one,flower,wherein,to,lie,curled,

Is,a,fiction,is,a,lie,
That,will,keep,God,in,the,sky.

46

It's,a,paper,face,you,have,
Said,the,saint,to,the,grave.

47

Throwing,diamonds,to,peacocks,
Is,a,philosopher's,prodigality.

48

Between,two,points,to,find,
Not,the,easy,straight,line,
But,the,Coil,of,Eternity.

49

Time,drunk—
Or,Time,creating,her,heroes.

50

A,hero,is,alive,and,is,made,dead.
The,correct,punctuation,
To,historical,grammar.

51

He,tries,me,Indoors,
Where,is,most,Sun.

52

Pierced! By,God,Supreme,Bullet!

CAPRICES

176

A Virginal

Well,then. And,a,v,virgin.
Well,then. And,a,y,virgin.
Well,then. And,a,z,virgin.

The,v,virgins,are,more,virtuous,
Than,the,z,virgins.
The,z,virgins,are,swifter,

For,their,z's,are,quicker.
The,y,virgins,are,shyest,youngest,
But,O,they,tell.

Well,then. And,a,y,virgin.
Well,then. And,a,z,virgin.
Well,then. And,a,v,virgin.

But,all,all,shall,become,x,virgins.

177

A,piece,of,coffee,a,piece,of,rose,
That's,all,for,breakfast,*that's,all!*

178

Moonlight's,watermelon,mellows,light,
Mellowly. Water,mellows,moon,lightly.
Water,mellows,melons,brightly.

Moonlight's,mellow,to,water's,sight.
Yes,and,water,mellows,soon,
Quick,as,mellows,the,mellow,moon.
Water,mellows,as,mellows,melody,
Moon,has,its,mellow,secrecy.

Moonlight's,moon,has,the,mellow,
Secrecy,of,mellowing,water's,water-
Melons,mellowly. Moonlight's,a,mellow,
Mellower,being,moon's,mellow,daughter.
Moonlight's,melody,alone,has,secrecy,
To,make,watermelons,sweet,and,juicy.

179

The,caprice,of,canteloupes,is,to,be,
Sweet,or,not,sweet,—

To,create,suspense. A,return,
To,Greek,drama.

Their,dramaturgy,is,not,in,the,sweet,
Soil,but,in,the,eye,

Of,birds,the,pure,eye,that,decides,
To,bestow,or,

To,withhold. Shall,I,be,sweet,or,
Not,sweet?—looking,

Up,at,your,face. Till,sudden:
I,will,be,sweet!

180

David,fourteen,fifteen,a,little,pepper,and,fox,
As,tall,as,tall,only,littler,only,bigger:
Enough,of,description.

In,this,green,morning,a,dot,in,the,center,it's,
Spring,remember,only,greener,only,newer:
Enough,of,the,season.

In,this,green,morning,David,fourteen,fifteen,a,
Littler,taller,a,littler,wiser,only,littler,bigger:
Spied,ah,Maryanne,

Ah,Maryanne,thirteen,fourteen,a,littler,golder,a,
Wiser,pepper,and,fox,only,lovelier,golder:
Ah,enough,of,enough.

181

A,cat,having,attained,ninehood,
Shall,fear,ninthhood!
A,rule,to,prove,catness,

Or,negation,of,cathood.

Catness,cats,and,nineness,proves.
Ninthless,cats,prove,
Immortal,cats.

Wherefore,Ninthhood,*is,*

Is,to,be,feared,
This,step,to,Ten!
So,cats,also,count,Ten.

The Emperor's New Sonnet

APHORISMS, II

53

Find,love,x,y,z,
Find,God,A,B,C.

54

I,was,nearly,mirror—
It,was,nearly,only,glass—

Till,in,the,room,together,
It,in,flesh,I,in,glass.

55

To,live,in,two,Forests,only!
How,difficult. How,lonely.

56

Suppose,a,little,monkey—
He's,a,sadder,thing,
Than,onions.

57

Any,hero,is,the,author.
Any,age,is,the,infant.

58

To,compose,a,ballet,of,
Ascetics—
Playing,with,matches!

59

Time,moves,from,left,to,right:
From,right,to,right:
From,right,to,left:
From,left,to,left:

Futurity.
Prophecy.
Remembrance.
Death.

60

A,capacity,to,hide,
Displayeth,every,germ,of,Truth.
Her,Columbus,must,be,
Adept,in,grand,geometry!
To,overtake,that,path,
Requires,giant's,stride.

61

Genius—
Snake,shedding,jewels:
Snake,shedding,immortalities.

62

The,circle,is,not,greater,
Than,its,radius,
Which,defines,its,genius.

The,tower,is,not,greater,
Than,its,altitude,
Which,defines,its,solitude.

63

The,Pure,Rebuttal.
Wherefore,we,devise,betrayal.

64

Birth,is,always,
Copying,from,immortality:
The,first,was,Lucifer—
The,rest,go,
By,the,name,of,Genius.

The,act,is,Trespass,
But,Life,forgives.

65

The,Chinese,have,a,way,
Of,being,Chinese,
Chinesely.

66

At,twelve,o'clock,the,poet,is,sad.
At,thirteen,o'clock,the,world,goes,mad.
At,mad,o'clock,the,hero's,blood.
At,blood,o'clock,the,shining,truth.
At,truth,o'clock,the,Timeless,Head.

67

Listen—
The,lovers',Tick-Tock.

68

To,count,fire,
In,dark,the,eyes,must,be:
The,visibility,is,of,jewels.

69

Not,all,birthdays,
Are,Inhabited.

70

Fade,out,fade,out,
Pale,spermless,God:
Arise,fire-testicled,God.

71

Tyrant,and,Tiger,and,
Divinest,Lover:

Therefore,thereto.

72

I,astonish,Death,with,my,largesse.
She,becomes,a,silly,maid,
Saying,"Never,mind. Never,mind."

73

The,man-eating,Word.

74

If,wisdom,can,not,count,
The,petals,of,a,snake,

Yet,wisdom,can,
Its,backbone,break.

75

True,God,is,lavish,death.
Any,hero,can,tell.
Any,brave,interrogatory,
The,same,answer,spell.
The,miracle,is,
To,startle,a,hero,with,death!

76

That,Clay,with,Axis.

77

Like,a,flower,seen,
Like,a,seen,flower,
Flowering,like,a,flower.

Such,is,the,great,face.
Great,the,face,of,such.
Face,greatly,such.

78

My,Fellowship,with,God—
My,University. Degree?
None. His,Fellows,go,
Unalphabeted.

79

God,I,do,not,love,—
Him,I,counterlove.

80

Success,is,defined,by,some,
In,terms,of,Dress—
By,poets: as,Peregrination,
To,Address.

81

Inlight.

82

A,division,of,mindhood,
Into,music,and,illumination—
What,death,cannot,take,hold,of!
A,confrontation,by,Manhood,
Of,the,ego,of,death.

83

Forehead,be,the,stair,
To,God's,dark,Atmosphere!

84

The,pleasure,of,history,
Is,its,knack,of,being,late:
To,arrive,a,ghost:
Or,the,metaphysics,of,success.

85

When,the,simplicity,of,mortality,is,not,seen,
The,difficulty,of,mortality,begins.

86

In,the,Pronoun,
Is,the,Word.

87

Brain,may,startle,with,
Reason's,brave,high,head:
But,Tilth,of,the,pith,
Defaulted,till,it,is,Christed.

88

When,Nothing,is,so,well,said,
Or,so,well,done,

It,betrays,itself,and,becomes,
Something:

As,apples,by,Cézanne,or,just,
Lines,by,Mondrian.

89

The,heart,is,not,Greek—
It,hath,no,unities.

90

How,clean,how,clear,how,manly,
How,cleancut,is,your,anger,
Like,the,tulip,athletic,flower.

91

The,Lord,hideth,well—
Yet,not,to,hide.
He,hideth,well,

To,make,Hero's,Lust.
To,make,His,heroes,last.

92

Two,is,*two*,because—
Mathematics,has,childhood,
With,a,maturity,of,
Exactitude.

93

There,is,a,poetry,of,shades,
As,exacting,
As,Braille,to,the,fingertips.

94

Personally,you,impersonally.
Liar!

95

The,littlest,love,is,a,big,affair.
The,tasking,is,immense.
The,danglers,at,this,verge,

Vault,vim,the,universe.

96

Knowledge—the,Edge,of,Yes,
Where,to,gnaw,too,much,
Is,to,reach,the,Edge,of,No.

97

Not,to,utter,wisdom,
But,to,shine,with,it,
Is,poetry's,ultimate,wit.

98

The,last,word,being,uttered,
The,next,is,not.
But,next,to,the,last,word,

The,not-word,summarizing,all.

from *SELECTED POEMS AND NEW* (1958)

AUTHOR'S NOTE

The poems in this book cover the years 1937–1957. The hitherto published poems are drawn from two previous collections: *Have Come, Am Here,** 1942, and *Volume Two,* 1949. I have here retained only those poems that I can still care about: meaning that, like it or not, a person matures and so does a poet: only that a poet's maturation also involves that of his craft, so that work written earlier, however true to his intellectual or spiritual vision, may later no longer please him for the simple reason that his sense of craft has further refined. Some poems, therefore, I have felt needed revision, and the extent of revision naturally depended on the particular poem.

The work accomplished since these volumes is in the section of New Poems and Adaptations. The Adaptations are conversions of prose into poetry: into poetic constructions: an experiment that has held my special interest since first trying it out in 1951. A further explication of their method will be found in the note preceding the group in the book.

I have appended a section of Early Poems, comprising what I deem to be the best of the work done in early youth. These poems have not had publication before and appear in print here for the first time.

The new poems are acknowledged to: *Botteghe Oscure, The London Times Literary Supplement, Poetry: A Magazine of Verse, Wake,* and *The Yale Literary Magazine,* where they first appeared.

JGV

---

* *Have Come, Am Here* appears in its original form in this centennial edition.

NEW POEMS AND ADAPTATIONS

Xalome

As,I,am,long,and,beautiful,
(Like,a,fish; like,a,rose)

As,I,am,young,and,masterful,
(Like,an,egg; like,a,typhoon)

As,I,am,wise,and,a,child,
(Like,a,vow; like,a,knife)

In,salamanders,of,ice,I,burn,
(Like,a,virgin; like,a,tear)

My,rebuke,of,John—
(Like,a,terminal,of,love):

Baptist,John's,head,then,shall,be,
(Like,a,kiss; like,a,church;

Like,a,beehive,in,the,sun)
My,beehive,in,eternity.

184

(Up)(in)(the)(Tree)

(Up)(in)(the)(tree)
(Whose)(eyes)(are)(blue)

(Lo)(a)(little)(bird)
(Whose)(flowers)(are)(gold)

(Up)(in)(the)(tree)
(Whose)(eyes)

(Lo)(a)(little)(bird)
(Whose)(flowers)

(Up)(in)(the)(tree)
(Whose)(flowers)(are)(three)

(A)(little)(bird)
(Whose)(eyes)(are)(true)

(Up)(in)(the)(tree)
(Who)(flowers)

(A)(little)(bird)
(Who's)(love)

185

*The Angel**

The,angel,is,an,
Intellectual,instrument,a,concept,of,
Impractical,and,in-
valuable,dimension. We,can,not,

Afford,his,diminution.
Pure,spirit,

The,elements,of,
Humanity,unmixed,in,him; yet,since,all,
Spiritual,truth,is,
Paradox—he,is,tender,and,
Terrible,our,safeguard,
Our,danger.

Science,measures;
Our,minds,follow,and,it,is,difficult,to,
Remember,the,magnif-
icent,and,frightening,stature,
Of,an,angel. We,unlock,
Space,make,ra-

dar,a,toy,but,it,
Was,our,ancestors,built,a,bridge,to,God:
The,morning,stars,sing,
Together! there,is,the,angel's,
Voice—there,is,
His,breath.

*Adapted from an essay by Mrs. von Erffa.

186

A Valentine for Edith Sitwell

Neglect,me,and,believe,me,and,caress,me.

A,sitwell,in,a,bird,
Is,all,eyes,no,word.
A,sitwell,in,a,rose,
Is,all,voice,no,door.
A,sitwell,in,a,pond,
Will,leave,ghosts,behind!

A,sitwell,on,a,leaf,
Will,rise,not,fall.
A,sitwell,on,an,unicorn,
Will,outdo,Gabriel's,horn.
A,sitwell,and,a,lion,
Will,toe,any,line.
A,sitwell,and,a,seven,
Will,truth,design.
A,sitwell,and,love,
Will,speak,a,tower:
                  Yet,
A,sitwell,and,a,child,
Will,dazzle,any,apple!

Neglect,me,and,believe,me,and,caress,me.

187

And,if,Theseus—then,Minotaur.
Coherence,and,severance,
By,the,seven,locks,of,strictness: by,diamond-law.
Bolt,me,more. Bolt,Him,more.
        What,brightfall,is,this—I,see,Him,
        In,the,eye,of,a,Tear.

To,mine,Him,deep—my,key-
Less,classic,my,labyrinth-
Word! Listener,exalter,startler—fullstrength,
My,vertex,rears,its,hazards,of,
        Eternity. By,ballot,of,the,real,
        Speak,my,Appoint,my,Key.

By,side,of,live,by,side,of,Taur,
Who,shall,alight,forth,tall,
Must,somersault,Him,gold! alight,Him,pure,
In,crystal,of,Original,Terror. My,

On-fire-standing,love—
Sustain,this,perilous,core.

Pythagor,Angel,rest,and,repeat.
Rest,and,repeat. Till,
With,the,gold-awaked,Verb,in,orience,lock—
Taurus,of,Minos,in,His,brightverb,sleep:
—With,wreck,all,East,
The,Vertical,complete.

188

The,Verb,in,its,Lair:
And,I—caught,
Caught,in,its,tick,and,tock:
Caught,in,its,rule,and,real:
At,last,
Divided,into,diamond.

There,in,the,east,air,
My,thistle,Verb,
My,gold,lightbreak! my,gale,Suez,
With,reals,and,reveals,of,love:
By,whose,
Exigent,fire: glitterer,

Tasker,perfect,rider:
I,man,each,
Poem,each,love. Here,in,
The,Faustdark,of,mortality,
Dig,dig,
The,clean,bones,of,reality:

And,ah—complexing,love,
Reversing,rose:
Thy,tidals,of,King-gold,erupt—

    (Noble,barbar,sweet!)
       The,nine-
    Living,ladders,of,eternity.

189

Death and Dylan Thomas

Gold,gong,of,
   Genius: continual,fire: leger,nobler,
   Of,lights. Genesis',fettled,dazer!
Gold-coilèd,Adam: dare-Adam,voice.
     Sleep,Dylan.
   Deity,began,you,giant—
     In,Plato's,curve,single:
   And,now,Death,greatlaw,great,
Kinglighter,his,right,hand,
Shines,your,name,the,whole,heaven,long.

Sleep,Dylan.
   Sleep,gentle,genius. Very,Death,saith:
   This,death,I,annul . . .
Eternity,bloodtells,him: O,
     From,his,lived-
   In,rose: into,life's,lifeline,
     Falcon-and-famous-verb,thrusts,him!
   And,exceller,beautiful,
Commandant,incendiar,oh,nightgold,
Forerunning,verb,myth-hard,he,stands.

190

The Anchored Angel

And,lay,he,down,the,golden,father,
(Genesis',fist,all,gentle,now)
Between,the,Wall,of,China,and,
The,tiger,tree (his,centuries,his,
Aerials,of,light) . . .
Anchored,entire,angel!
He,in,his,estate,miracle,and,living,dew,
His,fuses,gold,his,cobalts,love,
And,in,his,eyepits,
O,under,the,liontelling,sun—
The,zeta,truth—the,swift,red,Christ.

The,red-thighed,distancer,swift,saint,
Who,made,the,flower,principle,
The,sun,the,hermit's,seizures,
And,all,the,saults,zigzags,and
Sanskrit,of,love.
Verb-verb,noun-noun:
Light's,latticer,the,angel,in,the,spiderweb:
By,whose,espials,from,the,silk,sky,
From,his,spiritual,ropes,
With,fatherest,fingers,lets,down,
Manfathers,the,gold,declension,of,the,soul.

Crown,Christ's,kindle,Christ! or,any,he,
Who,builds,his,staircase,fire—
And,lays,his,bones,in,ascending,
Fever. Verb-verb,king's-spike—who,propels,
In,riddles! Six-turbined,
Deadlock,prince. And,noun,
Of,all,nouns: inventor,of,great,eyes: seesawing,
Genesis',unfissured,spy: His,own,Arabian,
His,love-flecked,eye!

The,ball,of,birth,the,selfwit,bud,
So,birthright,lanced,I,hurl,my,bloodbeat,Light.

And,watch,again,Genesis',phosphor,as,
Blood,admires,a,man. Lightstruck,
Lightstruck,into,the,mastertask,
No,hideout,fox,he,wheels,his,grave,of,
Burning,and,threads,his,
Triggers,into,flower: laired,
In,the,light's,black,branches: the,food,of,
Light,and,light's,own,rocking,milk.
But,so,soon,a,prince,
So,soon,a,homecoming,love,
Nativity,climbs,him,by,the,Word's,three,kings.

—Or,there,ahead,of,love,vault,back,
And,sew,the,sky,where,it,cracked!
And,rared,in,the,Christfor,night,
Lie,down,sweet,by,the,betrayer,tree.
To-fro,angel! Hiving,verb!
First-lover-and-last-lover,grammatiq:
Where,rise,the,equitable,stars,the,roses,of,the,zodiac,
And,rear,the,eucalypt,towns,of,love:
—Anchored,Entire,Angel:
Through,whose,huge,discalced,arable,love,
Bloodblazes,oh,Christ's,gentle,egg: His,terrific,sperm.

(190)

The Anchored Angel

And lay he down, the golden father
(Genesis' fist, all gentle now)
Between the Wall of China and
    The tiger tree (his centuries, his
    Aerials of light) . . .
              Anchored entire angel!
He, in his estate, miracle, and living dew,
    His, fuses, gold, his, cobalts, love,
        And, in his eyepits,
    O, under the liontelling sun—
The zeta, truth—the swift red Christ.

    The red-thighed distancer, swift saint,
    Who made the flower principle,
The sun, the hermit's seizures,
    And all the saults, zigzags, and
    Sanskrit of love.
          Verb-verb, noun-noun:
Light's latticer, the angel in the spiderweb:
    By whose espials from the silk sky,
        From his spiritual ropes,
    With fatherest fingers lets down,
Manfathers, the gold declension of the soul.

    Crown Christ's, kindle Christ! or any, he
    Who builds his staircase fire—
And lays his bones in ascending
    Fever. Verb-verb, king's-spike—who propels
    In riddles! Six-turbined
        Deadlock prince. And, noun
Of all nouns: inventor of great eyes: seesawing,
    Genesis', unfissured spy: His own, Arabian,
        His love-flecked eye!

The ball of birth, the selfwit bud,
So, birthright, lanced, I hurl my bloodbeat Light.

And watch again Genesis' phosphor, as
Blood admires a man. Lightstruck,
Lightstruck into the mastertask,
No hideout, fox, he wheels his grave of
Burning, and threads his
Triggers into flower: laired
In the light's black branches: the food of
Light, and light's own, rocking, milk.
But, so soon a prince,
So soon a homecoming, love,
Nativity, climbs him by the Word's three kings.

—Or there, ahead of love, vault back
And sew the sky where it cracked!
And, rared in the Christfor night,
Lie down, sweet, by the betrayer tree.
To-fro, angel! Hiving verb!
First-lover-and-last-lover, grammatiq:
Where rise the equitable stars, the roses of the zodiac,
And rear the eucalypt towns of love:
—Anchored Entire Angel:
Through whose huge, discalced, arable love,
Bloodblazes, oh, Christ's gentle egg: His terrific sperm.

The Anchored Angel appears here without commas—for the first time since September 17, 1954—when it was featured as the lead poem in *The Times Literary Supplement*, London, England, a special issue devoted to examining mid-century American poetry.

APHORISMS, III

99

Three,beautiful,dancing,dwarves,
Declare: "We,do. We,do. We,do.

"Rebellion,we,bid,you,do.
Euclid,upon,a,star,

"Shall,direct,your,pure,invisible,war."

100

A,nun,like,a,nun. A,Nun,
Who,will,become,a,nun.
A,bird! A,bird,already,an,egg.

101

A,genius,is,he,
Whose,*I*,
Can,generate,*us*.

102

The,sun,is,not,real.
The,sunshine,is,real.
But,the,sun,is,the,reality,
Of,the,imagination,of,the,sunshine.

103

Amaze,the,Sky,
With,the,Human,Verb.

104

Let,a,man,
Contain,an,angel. Yet,
Let,him,not,be,fully,angel,
Though,he,contain,
A,full,angel.

105

"To-whit! To-who!"
Sings,my,little,bird.

"To-*which*. To-*whom*!"
Chides,the,grammar-bird.

106

Reality,is,centric:
A,point,like,wit.

107

Tremendous,as,a,mere,world.
Tiny!
As,a,mere's,world.

108

Speak,in,the,dark.
What,the,light,believes,of,it,
Is,poetry.

109

When,I,say,As,if,a,
I,mean,As,if,the.
—That,is,very,difficult.

110

Learn,laws. Build,
A,great,theory's,rose.

111

The,biography,of,Infinity,
Is,little,enough,
Were,we,only,Child.
The,muscularity,and,the,terror,
Approach,us,only,
On,the,hill,of,age.
And,we,cry,"Wolf! Wolf!"

At,the,so,lovely,sheep.

112

If,a,rose,strikes—
What,would,you,do.

113

The,not-body,has,a,body.
The,not-spirit,has,a,spirit.
Beautiful,not-body,and,
Beautiful,not-spirit,
With,Body,and,Spirit,
One,Digit.

114

The,Lord,shoots,loneliness,
Without,a,sound.

115

Between,two,points,there,can,be,
    A,straight,line,
        A,curve,
            A,zigzag,
                A,spiral:
But,most,important,of,all,
The,mysterious,invisible,line.

116

On,with,the,sky!

117

Not,speech,that,has,fire,
But,Fire,that,can,speak—
Genius.

118

To,Afric,for,lions.

119

Whatever,can,happen,
Is,only,whatever,less,
Is,likely,to,unhappen.
And,it,can,be,happiness.
Which,can,fail,to,open,
Or,open,and,fail.

120

Commit,rose.
Or,
Commit,diamond.

121

Deny,him,help,
For,thou,art,
Angel,of,the,genius!

Divide,his,heart,
To,make,eternity,start.

122

Have,you,churches,to,sing?

123

At,last,I,learned,to,look,astutely,
Even,at,myself,looked,cunningly.
"Is,this,you?
Or,are,you,this?"

"This,is,I,but,I,am,you.
This,is,you,indeed,
And,I,indeed.
But,I,am,only,here,instead."

124

Skies,are,written,
Because,poems,are,born.

125

Hush! (snow-verb)

126

A,cat,chasing,its,tail—
A,circular,
Absurdity!
A,sudden,truth.

127

Abstract,as,a,Chinese,tear.

128

Until,awaking,is,
Not-awaking.
Until,then,is,tomorrow.
Between,is,future.

Yesterday,I,awoke,today.
The,future,was,involved.
Not-awaking,was,revoked—

I,awoke,absolved.

A NOTE ON THE ADAPTATIONS

The Adaptations are poems: from prose.

They are experiments in the conversion of prose, through technical manipulation, into poems with line movement, focus, and shape, as against loose verse.

The work, apart from the choice of material, has consisted mainly in constructing in verse what originally exists as prose. These adaptations spring from a diversity of sources: from published letters, journals, notebooks; as well as from sources the least expected to yield poems: magazine items and captions, letters to the editor, newspaper editorials, book reviews, even advertisements. In the choice of material one of course uses one's selective eye.

All the adaptations are in the words of their original texts. I have added nothing which cannot be found in them. On the other hand, in the interests of poetry and to achieve the tightness of verse, I have in some cases excised words (usually connectives or extra adjectives) or even whole phrases or clauses if inessential to my purpose. Punctuation has been altered to suit the movement of verse.

A few of these adaptations are Collages. I have borrowed the term from painting. The collages are adaptations where the sequence of the original text has been disturbed, where there has been, more or less, a pasting together. In the collage of the bullfight poem, for instance, taken from captions accompanying a photographic essay in *Life* Magazine, the sequence of lines is not as in the original text, but pieced together in a new order and made subservient to the ends of a poem. In another collage the poem derives from two different sections of a book yet achieves a unit effect.

In connection with this experiment of converting prose into poetry, William Carlos Williams has something pertinent to say in his *Selected Letters.* "Prose can be a laboratory for metrics. It is lower in the literary scale, but it throws up jewels which may be cleaned and grouped." This expresses very well what I tried to do.

JGV

ADAPTATIONS

191

When I Think of Rilke,

I see again that admirable
Handwriting, so marvelously penned
    Between Latin, and Gothic
In character. I say:

It seems as though he himself
Had written his whole destiny from
    The end of that pen! And
With that same hand

There is no action, no decision,
No love, no renunciation which
    He might not have signed
In its totality.

From the study by Edmond Jaloux in *Rilke:
His Last Friendship* (Philosophical Library).

192

This being-in-the-sun and
Breathing-in-spring-sky
And this listening to the little bird-
    Voices that are so well
      Distributed one feels how
In every spot in the air that
    Can bear one

—there is one! And however
Much I force myself to my
Desk, yet again and again I go with it:
The morning suddenly calls
Somewhere outside in a way
That makes one feel there must be
Another morning

Somewhere, a very big morning,
The morning of the seagulls
And of the island birds, the morning of
The slopes and of the
Inaccessible flowers: that
Ever the same eternal morning
That has not

Yet to reckon with human
Beings: who blink at it
Dubiously, mistrustfully; and one need
Only walk to have it really
Round one: the sea-
Morning that is sure everything
In it is with

It and nothing against it!
That in its opening its
Own gesture repeats itself thousands
And thousands of times,
Till it slows down in the
Little flowers and as it were
Collects itself.

From a letter to Clara Rilke. *Letters of Rainer Maria Rilke*, volume 1 (Norton).

193

The Allegory of the Cavern

One should see on the wall of the cavern
    A shadow of oneself corresponding
To the light of the fire;
    And having emerged

From it but still looking at the ground,
    A shadow of oneself, but produced
By the light of the sun . . .
    And an image of

Oneself in the water (level of mathematics
    And of love) . . . On lifting up one's
Head—one sees nothing
    More of oneself.

From *The Notebooks of Simone Weil*, volume 2 (Putnam).

194

The Admiration of Mountains

Strange confusion on the part
Of brains incapable of art,
    Between the lofty and
The beautiful. Switzerland: a
Wonderful reservoir of
    Energy: one has to go down
How far? to find abandon and

    Grace, laziness and voluptuousness
Again, without which neither
    Art nor wines is possible.
If of the tree the mountains
Make a fir—what

> They can do with man!
> Aesthetics and ethics of conifers.

From *The Journals of André Gide*, volume 1 (Vintage edition: Knopf).

195

> Everyone carries a room about
> *Inside him.* This
> Can even be proved
> By the sense of hearing. If
> Someone walks fast
> And one pricks up one's
>
> Ears and listens, say in the night,
> When everything round
> Is quiet, one hears, for
> Instance, the rattling of a
> Mirror not quite firmly
> Fastened to the wall.

From Franz Kafka's "First Octavo Note-book."
Wedding Preparations (Secker and Warburg).

196

> Think you must have it someday!
> This real wintergladness white
> In
> White and
> Soft and fresh—
> Or we must have it
>
> Together: must sit in a little
> Fur-covered sleigh: before us one
> Of
> The tall

Horses with
A three-belled chime;

And high over us now and then
The flick of a whip! And white
White
C o u n t r y
Roundabout, up,
And down and again high up

Into the distance. And blue behind
Or else a light glassy green in which
The
Pink of
A cloud is
Slowly turning to white.

From a letter to Clara Rilke. *Letters of Rainer Maria Rilke*, volume 1 (Norton).

197

The language of bells
Without clappers—heard
Incessantly throughout the
Nine months in which
Everyone is
Identical—

And yet mysteriously
Different: In this first
Tinkling melody of immortality
Lapping against
The snug and
Cosy walls of

The womb—we have
The music of the still-

Born sons of men—opening
Their lovely dead
Eyes one
Upon another.

From an essay by Henry Miller in one of his New Directions books.
I cannot locate the specific essay.

198

Death of Apollinaire

His small room was
Full of shadows and
Shadowy figures: His face

Illuminated the linen
On the bed. A laureate
Beauty! so radiant we thought

Of young Virgil: Death,
In Dante's robe, pulling
Him, as children do, by the hand.

From *The Journals of Jean Cocteau* (Criterion).

199

Dame Edith Sitwell Reading

Her entrance is a masterpiece.

She comes on slowly, almost
Reluctantly—it is not the
Majesty of movement, rather
The majesty of person that
Commands. Big, tall, rawboned,

With the face of a sensitive
Horse: she always wears an
Exotic robe: this one red
       Cut through with gold: and
At least one ring the size of

       A child's hand. She carries a
Massive, brocaded knitting
Bag and inevitably a white
       Flower. When she reaches the
Lectern—abruptly she changes

       Personality: puts aside
Exoticism as a quick-change
Artist discards a hat or
       Mustache! and becomes tweedily
English. Rummages through the

       Bag, discovering first her
Horn-rimmed glasses, which she
Sets on her magnificent nose—
       Then the books and loose
Papers that carry the poems she

       Intends to read. These last
Must be sorted and stacked
Before the reading can begin!
       But finally after a few
Pleasant words that smack of the

       English country house, the
Tweeds suddenly vanish into
The red-and-gold robe and Dame
       Edith begins to read . . . A two-
Way metamorphosis between

Chinese empress and Margaret Rutherford.

From an essay "The Poet as Player" by Gerald Weales.
New World Writing, Number 11 (New American Library).

200

Custom of the Leucadians

To hurl yearly, sacrifice to
Apollo,
A condemned Prisoner from the white

Rock, stuck with all sorts of
Feathers
Made into light wings, and many large

Birds tied about him to break
His fall:
And boats placed below to carry him

Out of the dominions if he
Survived.
Out of the dominions if he survived.

From *The Notebooks of Samuel Taylor Coleridge*,
volume 1 (item 1245) (Bollingen Foundation).

201

Mallarmé's Esthetic

Nothingness begins and ends
It: in the midst
Lies poetry. "Like the
Virgin space divided of
Itself in solitude"

The beginning is chaos and pure
Chance: "vanquished
Word by word": until
Nothingness and silence
Become "genuine and

Just." While the inner ear
Listens for the
Silences—of horror
And peace at either end
Of the eternity.

From the Introduction by Bradford Cook to *Mallarmé:
Selected Prose Poems, Essays and Letters* (Johns Hopkins).

202

Eleanora Duse

She is magnificent: expressing
Human things more greatly
Than any other individual—
Does not try
To make herself understandable,
She begins her gesture with
The being understood

And proceeds from there.
Says, shows, refuses to show
Herself, and right from the start
It is all one:
The whole: definitive of a
Higher order: as in the
Temple's pediment.

What magnificence and
What waste! No poet in all the
World and she is passing by. No
One was ever
In need of so much. So without
A stage, without an instrument,
She enlarges everyday

Life: quick provisional
Happenings come to themselves,
Transcend themselves, stand still,
            No longer fade
Away. And she is left upholding,
Unmoving, *overburdened*: because there
            Are never enough

Spectators to take from her
The fullness of her scene. Every
Next moment she is like a vineyard
            Already ripe
Again!—one would have to keep
Sending in laborers under the burden
            Of the grapes.

From a letter to Princess Marie von Thurn.
Letters of Rainer Maria Rilke, volume 2 (Norton).

203

That the absence of the sun
Is not the cause of Night—
        Forasmuch as this light is
            So great

It may illuminate the Earth
All over at once . . . but
        That Night is brought on
            By the

Influence of *dark* Stars—
That ray out darkness upon
        The Earth, as the Sun
            Does light.

From *The Notebooks of Samuel Taylor Coleridge*,
volume 1 (item 1000-I) (Bollingen Foundation).

204

... until the dark
Was changed into radiance—
One could see even the least
Things shining!—

But for all this
To happen, there must have been
Great winds; one must have lived
Through long nights

In which the storm
Was everything. Nights and days,
Veiled, half-lit, faint, like a
Delaying of the

Morning, merely until
Early evening, everything, even to that
Great still snowfall that fell
And fell and caused

The world to move more
Gently, the day to pass more
Noiselessly, and the night to come
More secretly ...

From a letter to Ellen Key. *Letters of Rainer Maria Rilke*, volume 1 (Norton).

205

To Become an Archer

To become an archer,
You should be for two
Years under a loom and not blink
Your eyes when the shuttle
Shoots back and forth:—

Then for three years
With your face turned
To the light, make a louse climb
Up a silk thread: When the
Louse appears to be

Larger than a wheel,
Than a mountain; when
It hides the sun: you may then
Shoot. You will hit it right
In the middle of the heart.

From Lao-Tse, quoted in *The Notebooks of Simone Weil*, volume 1 (Putnam).

206

In no sense can genius
Fail to be exceptional: Like
The jutting corner of a façade it

Reaches unexpected
Heights yet does not create vast
Wild spaces (exceptional!) nor

Does it know abandon
But maintains an assemblage of
Miniature shrines, colonnades,

Fountains—keeps them
As spiritual sites, so produces
A special and continuous palace.

From an essay, "Music and Literature," by Stéphane Mallarmé. *Mallarmé:
Selected Prose Poems, Essays and Letters* (Johns Hopkins).

207

The Golden Birds of Rimbaud

"The golden birds which flit through
The umbrage of his
Poems!" Whence came those golden birds
Of Rimbaud's? whither
Do they fly? Neither

Doves nor vultures; they inhabit
The airs. Private messengers
Hatched in darkness—released in the light of
Illumination. They bear
No resemblance to the

Creatures of the air—neither are they
Angels: Rare birds of
The spirit! birds of passage from sun to sun!
Not imprisoned in the
Poems: liberated there.

From Henry Miller, *The Time of the Assassins* (New Directions).

208

Do not be bewildered by the
Surfaces; in the depths
All becomes law.
And those who live
The secret

Wrongly and badly lose it only
For themselves: *and still*
Hand it on: like

A sealed letter: without
Knowing it.

From *Letters of Rainer Maria Rilke*, volume 2 (Norton).

209

The bullfight is pure art: the perfect
Bullfighter is fragile: man
Before brute, relying
On his skill, heart and
Courage—
The spectacle

Is all motion: motion, the perfection of
Motion: the breath-taking
Spectacle of one slim
Young man in a glit-
tering
Suit of lights,

Courting the deadly charges of the bull
With a slow and gentle
Grace. And in the
"Moment of truth" (the
Objective
Of everything

That has been done in the bull ring)—
Bull and bullfighter
Merge:—the bull's head
Down, the matador above
Him and
Death is there.

Collage. From an essay, "Beauty in a Brutal Art." *Life* Magazine, 1957.

210

The medieval tea-
Sipping ascetic Zen Buddhists drank
Tea simply to

Stay awake during
Their long hours of meditation.
Zen, who was

Their founder, was
Also their zenith: He sat nine years
In abstract

Meditation: sip-
ping tea, till his legs withered and
Fell off.

Collage. From *Life* Magazine, 1951.

211

If El Greco Was Astigmatic

Figures would have appeared
Elongated to him, but so
Would his canvas. If
He painted

Precisely as he saw, the ef-
fect would have been self-
Correcting. An astigmatic
May see a

Circle as an ellipse but
If asked to draw what

He sees he will draw
A circle.

From a letter to the editor. *Time* Magazine, March 24, 1958.

212

What stood there was
Nothing but a little house—
Overburdened with
An enormous thick roof that
Seemed commonplace;
But of which
The angels perhaps

Knew that it had the
Right measurements: those
With which they measure
The great space surrounding
It: like the smallest
Part of that
Endless scale

The unit of measure:
Which keeps recurring and
With which one can
Reach to the end without
Adding anything else
But the same
Thing over and over.

From a letter to Clara Rilke. *Letters of Rainer Maria Rilke*, volume 1 (Norton).

213

Not all who would be are
Narcissus. Many

Who lean over the water
See only a vague

Human figure. Genet sees
Himself every-
Where! The dullest surfaces
Reflect his image;

Even in others perceives
Himself: bringing
To light their deepest
Secrets. The disturb-

ing theme of the Double.
The Image. The
Counterpart. The Enemy
Brother is found.

From the foreword by Jean-Paul Sartre to Genet's *A Thief's Journal*.

214

Certain Indians of high
Mountain country where
Neither mirrors nor
Water-pools are known

Recognize other natives
In a group photograph
But do not recognize
Themselves. They ask

Who "the strangers" are
But they can at least
Make out that these
Are pictures. Whereas

There are peoples who
    Cannot even do that
        And will look at a
            Photograph upside down.

From Jean Cocteau, *The Hand of a Stranger*.

215

The Storm

    A storm came up,
    Black bodied, from the sea: bringing
Rain and twelve winds to drive
      The hill birds off
      The face of the sky—

    The storm, the black
    Man, the whistler from the sea bottom
And the fringes of the fish
      Stones, the thunder,
      The lightning, the mighty

    Pebbles, these came up!
    As a sickness, as an afterbirth, coming
Up from the belly of weathers;
      The antichrist from
      A sea flame or a steam

    Crucifix, coming up
    The putting on of rain: the multiply-
ing storm, the colour of temper,
      The whole, the unholy,
      Rock handed, came up coming up!

From a story, "The Lemon," by Dylan Thomas.
Adventures in the Skin Trade (New American Library).

216

And then suddenly,
A life on which one could
Stand. Now it carried one and
            Was conscious of one while it
Carried. A stillness in which
            Reality and miracle

Had become identical—
Stillness of that greatest
Stillness. Like a plant that is to
            Become a tree, so was I
Taken out of the little container,
            Carefully, while earth

Ran off and some light
Came to my roots; and was
Planted in my place for good, there
            Where I was to stand, until
My old age, in the great,
            Whole, real earth.

From a letter to Clara Rilke. *Letters of Rainer Maria Rilke*, volume 1 (Norton).

217

And I said to myself
I will no longer be the reflection but
            That which is above:
            And I

Turned myself over so
That I was no longer upside down, and
            Closed my eyes for a brief
            Moment

And drew myself about
Me and stretched my contours as one
Stretches violin strings
Until

One feels them taut and
Singing! And suddenly I knew I was
Fully outlined like a Dürer
Drawing.

From a letter to Clara Rilke. *Letters of Rainer Maria Rilke*, volume 1 (Norton).

218

You would not say
Along that road
The sea was there behind
The houses: behind
The fir trees and the hedge,
And the apples getting ripe.
And yet,
Round the bend,
The sea is there.

He has entered at
One stride into
The land! Union of the
Vast and lonely with
The little houses,
The land, the little harbor—
Like
Milton standing by
A little door.

From a letter to John Hall Wheelock. *The Letters of Thomas Wolfe* (Scribner).

219

And when what is near
You is far—then your
Distance is
Already among the stars.
And very large.

Rejoice in your youth
In which you can take
No one with you!
And be kind to those who
Remain behind.

From the *Letters of Rainer Maria Rilke* (Norton).

220

Strindberg

At first it seems
So hopelessly obstinate to present
Humanity's disconsolation
As its absolute

Condition. But when
Someone like this has power over
Even the most disconsolate,
There hovers above

The whole—unspoken—
A concept of illimitable human
Greatness. And
A desperate love.

From a letter to Princess Marie von Thurn. *Letters of Rainer Maria Rilke*,
volume 2 (Norton).

221

More single-purposed than
The new bird: all mouth with his
One want: your son

Does not step down out of
His hammock but to collect his
Own apple with his

Own sin. As his son too,
And his son's son, shall do at
The proper time.

Collage. From Elizabeth Smart, *By Grand Central Station I Sat Down
and Wept* (Poetry London).

222

Death of Raymond Radiguet

(in his own words to Jean Cocteau)

"In three days
    I shall be shot,
        By the soldiers of
God. The order has been

Given: *I heard
    The order.* . . .
        There is a colour that
Moves and people hidden

In the colour.
    You cannot send
        Them away, as you
Cannot see the colour."

Quoted in Margaret Crosland, *Jean Cocteau* (Knopf).

223

Night and sleep alone
Permit metamorphoses. Without
Oblivion in the
Chrysalis the caterpillar
Could not

Become a butterfly: The
Hope of awaking someone else
Urges me to let
The man I am to sink in-
to sleep.

From *The Journals of André Gide*, volume 2 (Vintage edition: Knopf).

224

Dr. Vilhjalmur Stefansson

Learned the Arctic by
Becoming an Eskimo for
Ten winters. Housed in

An igloo, foraging from
An ice-floe, dining on
Caribou skin and

Seal oil, he still saw
The North with an
Optimist's eye. "This,"

Said Dr. Stefansson, "is
No hostile icecap but
A friendly, fruitful

Land of vast promise."
Men listened: new
Cities sprang up,

New air routes bridged
The Land of the
Midnight Sun.

From an advertisement of the Lockheed Aircraft Corporation
that appeared in national magazines, 1956.

225

Military History,

Like war itself, is much too
Serious to be left to
Military men. The
Generals could

Write it well enough if it
Were only a matter of
Brass-bound decisions and
Their results in

Defeat or victory. But
Military history is
Also concerned with
Men's minds and

Emotions—politics, patriotism,
The smell of death,
And what songs
The soldiers sang . . .

From a book review by Orville Prescott of *Gallipoli* by Alan Moorehead.
New York Times, Sept. 17, 1956.

226

The early Chinese probably
Encountered a fungus highly
Hallucinogenic: Though
        It has disappeared from
                The soil
It survives in the form of
A scepter

        Usually fashioned of carved
Jade but may be of gold,
Ivory or rare wood: called
        Ju-i which means "As
                You would
Wish." Given to members of
Nobility

        On special occasions or to
Important visiting high
Officials, Taoists claim
        Anyone lucky enough to find a
                Ju-i
Will have a glimpse of
Paradise.

From a letter to the editor. *Life* Magazine, June 3, 1957.

227

Characters in Historical Novels

Express emotion by
        Changing color from
                Pink to grey,
Scarlet, dull red and
Glistening chalk
White until

The reader feels like
The chameleon—said
To become a
Nervous wreck when
Nudged across a
Plaid bedspread.

From a book review in *Time* Magazine, Feb. 17, 1958.

228

The Manner of a Poet's Germination

is less like that of a bean
in the ground
than a waterspout at
sea. He has to
begin as a cloud

of all the other poets he ever
read: and first
the cloud reaches down!
toward the water
from above, and then

the water reaches up! toward
the cloud from
below—and finally cloud
and water join
together to roll as

one pillar between heaven and
earth: the base
of water he picks from
below, all the life
he lived outside of books.

From a talk by Robert Frost. Quoted in *Beloit Poetry Journal*, chapbook no. 5.

229

Through what twists and
Transformations
We recognize the same logical form;
Consider the similar-
ity of

Your two hands . . . Put one,
Palm down, super-
impose the other, palm down—they
Are not alike at all,
Are exact

Opposites: their respec-
tive shapes fit
The same description modified by a
Principle of ap-
plication

Whereby the measures are
Used one way for
One hand, the other way for the
Other . . . like a
Timetable

In which the list of
Stations is marked
"Eastbound . . . read down;—
Westbound . . .
Read up."

From Susanne K. Langer, *Problems of Art* (Scribner).

230

Mondrian

Pruned his palette to
    Primary colors and his
        Design mechanisms to
Verticals and horizontals;—
    Finally he

Reached a point at which
    He could not abide
        Green and changed seats
At tables to avoid
    Seeing trees:

This magician who in
    His early work did some
        Of the most sensitive
Studies of trees ever achieved:
    Advancing

The degree of abstraction
    From example to
        Example until they
Vanished in squares and
    Rectangles.

From a book review by Howard Devree of *Piet Mondrian* by Michel Seuphor.
New York Times Book Review, 1957.

231

Nyabongo's Project

One of the strangest projects is
That of Dr. Akiki Nyabongo, an

East Indian prince residing in
          Brooklyn. Ebito's historian, a handsome
          Liquid-eyed man of forty-two, is a prince
                    By virtue of
                    Being a son of the late

          Kyebambe, King of Toro, a state
          In Uganda, and a doctor by
Virtue of a Ph.D. at Oxford. He
          Was born in Kabarole, Toro's capital,
          In the shadow of the Ruwenzori Moun-
                    tains, sometimes
          Known as the Mountains

          Of the Moon. Dr. Nyabongo is
          Preparing a book about Ebito
Or Flower Language, a symbolic
          Method of communication among his compatriots,
          Involving the use of flowers, leaves,
                    Grass, seeds, twigs,
          Clay, beads, animal hair and

          Stones. He is engaged in setting
          Down detailed scientific des-
criptions of plants which he
          Will then key to their messages in Rutoro
          And English. A typical one: "Akaisabi-
                    sabi, or Aspa-
          ragus puberulus. A much-branched,

          Climbing shrub. Branches long,
          Flexuose, terete; branches long,
Spreading . . ." means "You are the
          Puberulus that grows at the side of the road
          And grasps the bark cloth of every
                    Passerby, and
          I will grasp at your love."

Collage. From an item in "Talk of the Town." *New Yorker*, Jan. 26, 1952.

232

British painter Ben Nicholson
Made a pilgrimage to
Mondrian's quiet,
    Immaculate Paris studio over-
      Looking the Montpar-
        nasse rail-

road tracks—and likened it to
"One of those hermit's
Caves where lions
    Used to go to have thorns
      Taken out of
        Their paws."

From an item in *Time* Magazine, June 24, 1957.

233

The brotherliness and
The darkness of God. So I
Named him, the God who had broken in
    Upon me: and I lived
    A long time
In the anteroom of his name,

On my knees. Scarcely
Now would you ever hear me name
Him: between us indescribable discretion:
    Where once was nearness,
    Penetration—
There stretch new distances

As in the atom: instead of
Possession, relation: a name-

Lessness that must begin again with
God to be complete
And without
Evasion: attributes taken

Away from God!—the
No longer expressible—fall
Back to creation, to love and death . . .
Out of the breathing
Heart, with which
The sky is covered.

From a letter to Ilse Jahr. *Letters of Rainer Maria Rilke*, volume 2 (Norton).

234

Man's Fate

You know the phrase—
"It takes nine months
To make a man; and
A single day
To kill him."

Listen: it does not
Take nine months—it
Takes fifty years to
Make a man.
Fifty years of

Sacrifice, of will,
Of so many things . . .
And when this man is
Complete, when
There is nothing

Left in him of child-
hood nor adolescence,

When he is really a man,
        He is good for
        Nothing but to die.

From André Malraux, *Man's Fate* (Modern Library).

235

The Woman

But the woman, the woman:
She had completely collapsed
Into herself: forward

Into her hands. . . . The street
Was too empty: it caught
My step from under my feet.

The woman startled: pulled
Herself away too quickly!
Out of herself too violently—

Her face remained in her two
Hands—its hollow form
A face from the inside—

From Rainer Maria Rilke, *The Notebook of Malte Laurids Brigge* (Norton).

236

The Bird

A little bird that is thirsty:
        One takes it away from
The verge of death: its little heart
Beats increasingly

        Against the warm, trembling hand,
        Like the last wave of

A gigantic sea whose shore you are.
And you know suddenly,

With this little creature that
Is recovering, that
Life is recovering from death! And
You are holding it up,

Generations of birds and all
The woods over which
They fly and all the heavens to which
They will ascend.

From a letter to Otto Modersohn. *Letters of Rainer Maria Rilke*,
volume 1 (Norton).

237

First frost comes,
Back in the hills, and the fox
Barks in the thin
Moonlight;
The owl asks

Its questions of the
Darkness.—Autumn creeps in,
Reconnoitering the
Valleys,
Exploring

The treetops. Cricket
And katydid, silent in the first
Frosty evening,
Return
As the chill

Abates. . . . Thus turns
The season, in ripeness and morn-
ing mist, in mid-
day sky
So deep, so clear.

From a *New York Times* editorial, 1956.

238

Neither beginning nor end—
To the imagination: but it
Delights in its
Own season—

Reversing the usual order at
Will. Of the air in the
Coldest room it will
Seem to build

The hottest passions—Mozart
Danced with his wife, whis-
tling his own tune to
Keep the cold

Away! And Villon ceased to
Write upon his Petit Tes-
tament: only when the ink
Was frozen.

From William Carlos Williams, *Kora in Hell* (City Lights Books).

EARLY POEMS

LYRICS

239

The Coconut Poem

The coconuts have ripened,
They are like nipples to the tree.
 (A woman has only two nipples,
 There are many women-lives in a coconut tree.)
Soon the coconuts will grow heavy and full:
I shall pick up one . . . many . . .
 Like a child I shall suck their milk,
 I shall suck out of coconuts little white songs:
 I shall be reminded of many women.
. . . .
I shall kiss a coconut because it is the nipple of a woman.
             (Age 17)

240

Poem for Violeta

Your name is a cool word: even as brookwater.
It is quiet like a young bird: under a green leaf.
Cool as brookwater, quiet as a young bird:
Your name falls from my lips.
It is thus you do not hear it called from these lips:
Your name is a cool word, quiet like a young bird.

241

I demand brilliance and
Consecration. Because of a star.
How beautiful is the night like
Grass! Love is not far
Nor your hand.
              This being so
Love me well, love me well.
Because what Love is
I saw.
      I saw Love well:
Love tied a bell
To your heart. Love said, Kiss
Him and let your heart ring.
And this is the thing.

242

Poems for an Unhumble One

I

But the leaves and you are proud—
so no.
      It is summer now and did they
have you.
          So then
          when
          and if you can.
And a rose was bought:
it was as never and as still.
                The doves
came: they too were proud.
      The cherries and the bees: but these
were meek.

I asked forgiveness
until lost.

II

There was no end and how young.
I could not say it because there.
And how never yet seen for peace.
But it was there and bright like dark.
I touched it not, for love.

III

And still. As all is silver now,
how could. The roses gone and
but a pagan left. Too young and
resurrected.
            I did place at
the feet, love. In leaves.
      I did bow.
Was rain. Did she her fingers
the leaves unfold?
            It is
told: A pagan left. Too young
and resurrected.

IV

As if and when: and so I speak
of the waters of.
                  I am not of mountains
nor of rivers and yet.
But the brook of my body. And on your
breasts.
      The windness of.
Could I but. And as I am was.
      There were not as if and when
of which I speak. Of the darkness which.
      Victoring slew.

V

And this and all these and all of:
because of roses, Jesu.
                    I did
place at the feet—remembereth?
love. In leaves.
                    And could I but.
Yet I did bow.
I did arise from
                    tenderness: I touched
                        not: I silvered
                            love.

243

This second is more
        Than the hour—
This midget minute
        The little pebble

That felled Goliath!
        The little sob
That broke and
        Ended boyhood—

The secret rose
        In the Eve-face
That sets all boy-body
        In typhoon!

244

If Addition were Subtraction,
Then 'twere Love.
A sum of paradox

To audit incomprehends
And best in locks.

A littlest segment so vast,
And vastest segment
The littlest dole,
The comprising which
Is Immortality's segment and whole.

Mathematicus built it so,
Locking secret
Into strangest Arc,
The which to add were to subtract,
To subtract—to excel the Mark.

245

Love Song

And I do much love thee
and I will not leave thee not
answer me I being bright
and foreverly

Dear love brightcurvely most
dear love strew rosely flame
bravely to reach me and

starkly wind fingers gracely
deeply undeathing birds
luminous endlessly

Breathe me love I do much
love thee and of me bright
musical lyre dazzle god-
beauteously foreverly

life

246

Curve of gold above her
In the golden night,
Seventeen times I rose
Creating our child.

Seventeen kisses she gave me
In that golden night,
Seventeen times I rose
Creating our child.

Seventeen times I sang her
In that golden night,
Seventeen times I rose
Creating our child.

Seventeenth lift of gold,
Seventeenth fall of love,
In her golden soil
Sowen sweet our child.

247

Fragment

Now lies she quiet, quiet,
Like moonlight by him.
Quiet. Quiet. Knowing
His jewels are in her.
Quiet. Quiet. Knowing
He is quiet but will
Arise again. Quiet. Quiet.
But he will arise again.

248

How beautiful is sleep. Let
the young lover sleep.
     After her deep
let the young lover sleep.
     After the river
after the fever
he has been giver
    He has been true
he has been swift
make him now this gift:
     Let the young
lover sleep.
How beautiful the young lover in sleep.

249

O lovely thighs
O enbrought to God's ken.
The maiden's menses broken
By Love's surprise.

The rubies forestalled.
The rubies enjailed
That never had failed
Till Love had called.

O sweet Inflictive.
O holy and holy
O august
Superb Annunciative.

250

One hemisphere the heart,
Another the mind,
The two one World
But one is blind—

The heart so dim,
The mind so clear,
Weathers so different
Though of One Father—

Who willed a world so parted:
Point and counterpoint,
Poise and counterpoise,
Balanced noble at His finger's point.

251

The r
ed rose withereth
that I have put in a v
ase of cool w
ater.

The r
ed rose withereth
that I have put in a v
ase of cool w
ater.

252

Q. And did you see Wisdom?
A. Yes, I saw her, the August One!
Q. Did she bid you welcome?

A. Why, yes, and in a most cordial tone.
   But as I gazed at her upon her throne
   And saw no lover, not a one,
   I felt immediately undone.
   And then I ran . . .

I ran and ran from the Divine One.
I was glad again to feel the earthly sun.
For though she was most beautiful,
Upon her throne so impeccable—
O her lovely feet! naked
And music-shaped,
These were upon a human brother's skull.

253

Religionist! you up-down there,
You are so never

You never see how pitiful is God.
You praise him

Who needs no praise—but a mouth
Over his mouth

A voice beside his voice. You praise,
You praise only!

254

The Nude is to be viewed.
Do not exclude
Nor young nor old.
A nude is handsomest gold.

A male nude.
And see what he doth include

Betwixt his thighs:
His terrible and wise.

A female nude.
And see what she doth include
Betwixt her thighs:
Her perfect surprise.

These nudes are us
If we are precious!
These nudes are pure
And will endure.

255

All saints are naked (how
terribly true) they sit on

grass and play with mice
(how terribly, terribly nice)

All saints are naked (how
terribly wicked) they sit

on grass and play with mice.
Delight is such a little term

for such a lovely view!

256

Will you always for I can always.
It is so beautiful to know.
I do always know how always I can
Though never you sing my praise.

Yet upon such only shown, such only
As sun upon its only throne.
But always to sun there is to always can
To always can flawlessly.

So I do always know alwaysly
Your flawless grace and glow.
And however lawlessly you speak
You speak from an always throne

And your alwaysness the loveliest Greek
Since flawless Helen shone faithlessly.

257

There was a perfect tree.
There was a perfect fruit.
Around it curled
Beautiful Lucifer!

There was a perfect man.
There was a perfect woman.
But beautiful Eve
Passioned for the fruit.

Beautiful Lucifer held it.
Beautiful Eve took it!
The perfect woman
Passed the fruit to Adam.

Beautiful Lucifer hid now!
Beautiful God wrathed now.
Adam and Eve
Birthed the world now.

258

Complexity's unity—
That is Simplicity.

To be simple in
The uncomplex

Is no attainment.
The compliment is in

The complex achieving
The slender musical vertex.

PHILOSOPHICA

259

All in the name of you whom I love
Terribly not.
Therefore I love you.
I love you very undearly.
I love you most impossibly.

Then the marriage of our true minds must
Certainly be not.
Therefore we must get married.
We must get married in great delay.
We must get married as soon as not possible.

And as soon as the year is not over
To unname the child
And unbaptize him for his dear sake.
We will give a party for whoever
Will not be there.

260

The preliminary is the beginning dissolution.
The skeleton is final.
The desolation is royal.
Chemistry will indefine all solution
As it will define all insolution.

Or very nearly until the end has ceased
To be an end and become a major beginning.
Instruction here promotes prophecy.

And the skeleton in adultery
Is the trick called eternity.

261

Exactly what is unexact
In unexactness is exact:
Exactness unstatic,
Precision elastic.

What princelier fact
Exhibits subtler tact
Than this exactness
Of subtle unexactness?

262

When God my darling turned adulterous
I knew Who and When.
Since I loved I forgave.
Since I forgave I could not forgive.

For He was beyond forgiving, being God,
However adulterous.
Since He was so, He forgave.
Since He forgave He could not forgive.

And we were at a standstill—
God and I and forgiveness at a standstill.
Until I knelt to Him I could not forgive
Until He knelt to me He could not forgive.

And the lesson of it is very great
And that is "How beautiful is hate."

263

Observe me. I do not speak.
But I am very quick
And already I have spoken.
Observe me as now I speak.
But I am very quick
And already I have unspoken.

264

From the beginning it has been the ending.
From the beginning it has been end-conjuring.
From the beginning we move dispersing
To the unity of the end.

The soul knows
What it cannot know.
It knows
Where it cannot go.
It knows
It like a quiet law
It knows
It and does not know.

Knowledge of the unknowledge!
The mind at the obscure ledge
Of Beginning-Ending. The mind
Reaching forward to reach Behind.

265

The standstillness of unthought
Into the fury of thought:
The mind, perceptor,
Becomes preceptor.

And maddens to establish boundaries
Say, This is thought
This not thought . . .

But it is Unthought all the time,
The Diamond,
Each facet of which is thought.

266

If it is again futurity
It is only until.
Or nearly so.
If it is to be undressed
It is only transposition
From now to then
Or no to yes.
What becomes clearly unseen
Is the great sheen
Of so much energy
The dramaturgy of which
Nowness bewitches.
Its noneness charms!
Its clownness mocks.
Or nearly until.

267

I am earlier than today
And transpose Futurity
To Now.
Eventually will come Later
But I made it now.

Transposer announcing
So no later marvelling.

The Future to me is Now
For I came earlier.

My earliness can picture
Your mouths corruptive.
If you adore lateness
Earliness is nothing.
Punctuality of lateness
Being Now-decomposing.

268

Now is the speech of Tomorrow
In certain mouths.
A certain Ghost is Eternity
Who, as we walk herward,
Walks usward,
Speaks nowward.

Un-ears and un-eyes
Stand in disbelief and surprise.
The law of their clock is riven.
The law of their orbit is broken.
This speech is misshapen!
Wherefore, sharpen sharpen

Your claws O fellow citizens:
You have work to do
You have crosses to rear
You have history to smear.

269

Looking into the least mirror
The face should crack
Did not the ego hold it up together!
And seeing it whole we pause

To venerate that face—

The art of vanity is the
Putting a broken face together
A no-face into semblance of face
The not-portrait so lifelike!

The art of the mirror is
To not-crack with anger or laughter
To suffer image-infliction
With humility
And even join the eyes'
Chorus of approbation.

270

A certain morning is
Any morning with
A certain event.
Any morning is uncertain
Until that event.
And the event itself uncertain
Until it has passed uncertainty.

Such a morning is certain then
And reference can be made to it.
As the Creation Morning
Whose certainty has lapsed to uncertainty.
Or the Day for Doom
Whose uncertainty has lapsed to certainty.

Any certain morning
Lavishes joy or mourning.
Any uncertain morning
Does the same.
Certainty and uncertainty
Two sides of the same flame.

271

My portrait is my not-face
My portrait has this grace:
Where is your portrait
That has no face?

Your faces have no portraits
My portrait has no face:
Between your face and my face
God's portrait graciously waits.

Where are your beautiful portraits?
Your portraits without faces?
What is a portrait
If it is only a face.

272

When what cannot run runs
What is run is not run:
It is not poetry and its resemblance
Is the wrong countenance.

That which is real runs a distance
Beyond unrunning; at its
Onset is already there.
This alone is poetry.

And what it has run has no
Unravelling, however one may try.
Its countenance is sure and firm:
Itself its only resemblance.

273

Your profundity is very light
My lightness is very profound.
How so?
Impossible to know.

Difference is in the difference.
Impossibility to know
But with the straightest inference
Of the vital difference.

Not known, not defined,
Not even outlined.
But as your profundity moves
Itself disproves.

Now my lightness plays
And ends to amaze:
And the amaze is profound
Over my peculiar ground.

from *APPASSIONATA:*
POEMS IN PRAISE OF LOVE
(1979)

To a Lady Going to Antipolo

In Antipolo there will be many young men who will
come to you. You will like them because their tongues
will be honeyed and their feet light. You will forget me.
I shall be forgotten by you whom I cannot forget.

As you forget me I shall tap my fingers on my breast,
calling for you.

I shall talk to you through trees, through the arms of
dancers, through sweet words uttered by many lovers.

The arms of dancers round you shall be my arms.

The eyes of men admiring you shall be my eyes.

I have many arms, many eyes.

It is that, loving you, I have become many lovers.

In fancy, because I do not want other men's
arms about you, I have made the many dancers
myself.

As they clasp you round the waist, it shall be I holding
you.

The words of love they shall tell you are not theirs but
mine.

I am many lovers.

For you, if you also love me, you will find me in many dancers, in their bodies, in their words.

I am many lovers because I love you.

275

To ensnare a proud love
The heart must keep cool, keep cool;
Not the heart must move
To ensnare a love so beautiful.

The heart must keep still, keep still,
Austere as stalactite;
Her tiptoe upon the hill
Welding delight with fright.

Poised like a diamond arc
Within the reaving breast,
The heart must aim its mark
(Proud love, proud love addrest!)

With firmest, stoic hand.
Fly its arrow without sound
Till it prove imperial command
Or perish splintered on the ground.

276

Fulfilment

I cannot tell it to you the way it
should be told.
Have I yet told you tales? poems?
I have only songs, which I cannot

tell to you—
My voice is yet so young.

Let me be older,
Let my arms be stronger,
Let my lips learn the song of love—
Then I shall be ready.

I have learned the poem of kiss,
beloved.
Shall I tell it now to you?

"Yes, my lover."

But I am kist unto death!

277

Story

This is lovely:
   She asked him to love her: to touch her:
   to take of her: all: till his thirst was
   quenched—and he took.

This is lovelier:
   When he was through he lay quiet: cool
   as brookwater.

This is loveliest:
   Arising, he took her face in his hands,
   and closed her lids gently, and gave her:
                  the
                  last
                  kiss.

278

Have I Sung?

i

Lift me up: touch me: look at me.
I will sing.

ii

Have I sung?
Have I become soft, beautiful?

iii

You have become soft, beautiful.

iv

I have sung.

279

Descriptional

I could hear it like a flower
                              (like
a curve of rose).
I could touch it like sun
                         (like love).
It was very there and so very fair.
It was very bright and so very white.

Thus I strove for love . . . O
I could touch it, I could feel it.
                              I could feel it

like a stab of sun. I could hear it
like a flower, like a curve of rose:

Then a dove came down in sunshine!

280

Song for the First Sweetheart

Surely, O my love,
you are come
singly
on white footsteps—

Surely, O my love,
poised
on your hands
you carry the song
of the first embrace—

And on your lips, love,
surely you have hid
the kiss
that is to reach
all of myself—

Surely, surely, love,
these bring
to your first lover
and the last.

281

Pastorale

We loved well. This
I can tell.

Her eyes

O they were dark,
her hair O as the
                              very-dark.
Birdly cooed she
birdly O birdly
                    to me.
Leafly her mouth
folded to a kiss,
                         leafly
O leafly in bliss.
But it was this
                    told me
how much I was
loved: so fairly,
                         so fairly
fell she to a sleep,
to a sleep—
                    bird of
love my name
on her lips.

282

As of Tulips: As of Two Lips

It will not: it will really never.
It is said so: it is said low.
Love has a way of tall grace.
As of tulips: as of two lips.
And a peacock is only love
grown proud.
As of tulips: as of two lips.
So then let her pride abide.

Before love grew proud O did love
glow bright.
And there it is said.

As of tulips: as of two lips.
Love has a way may not be said.
It is said so: it is said low.
It will not and it will really never.

283

Lotus

She has gone to the waters of the blue-breasted river.

There she will pick a lotus, and still one other lotus, and still one other one: three loti shall know the splendour of her hands.

She will come bringing me three loti: she will come bringing her lover three loti: she will come bringing her lover three splendours.

The first splendour—the splendour of love over her eyes.

The second splendour—the splendour of love over her breasts.

The third splendour—the splendour of love over her thighs.

And when she shall have given me her three loti, she shall have known the three splendours: she shall have become the Eternal Lotus.

284

Go to a woman and say to her:
I want to live with you . . .

Drop to her feet for she is young

and most fair,
Touch her not yet, while her eyes
        receive you.

Down the road of her eyes,
        your young fairness shall go,
Down to the last petal of her heart
        she shall receive you.

Gaze at the white flower of her breasts
        (cruel, sweet tenderness!)
But touch her not yet, while her eyes
        receive you.

Ai! she is young and most fair, her hands
        in your hair
Fear her not now, O touch her well now!
        she has received you.

285

Duetto for Surrender

To you
who are rosed with d
arkness,
        love—
To you
who are softer than m
oonlight,
        love—
Surrender, my virgin,
be dark
        O be dark!

—I
surrender, love.
        I am taken

O am taken
by the victory of s
urrender,
   love!

286

Blossom Under Thee

And no leaves falling, love?
and no petals breaking
and no dew lost?

            And the
moon young and a star
old and speaking love?

And thou wilt come over me
white as moonlight
sharp as a star and a blade:

          and I
blossom under the moonlight
blossom under thee, love
thou wilt be gentle, wilt thou

not be, love?

287

Poem Written Beneath a Blue Lampshade

I speak this poem tenderly
it being for you
          and

for you only.—We were not
afraid and we did take love
gorgeously

We had no fears

We knew love we knew it and
we were dancers for it

and also
we were rivers we were moonlight
and also we were winds
as also

we were gods. And all this
is remembrance and all this
is desire

But also it is love

288

Come, Wreathe Me with Love

Come, wreathe me with love, beloved,
Scatter my breast on thy bed.

Be I a brook a-curl on thy grass,
Be I young, dark, and white as glass.

Be thou a blue bird, be thou a hunter
Look for the lovely delta, fragranter

Than love and her roses. Look thou for sun
Look thou for star, time can not run

Lovelier than on the breasts of love.
Prince of desire, O blue bird above,

Straighten thy arrow: pierce and be found:
Love shall be served, music resound.

289

Twin Poems

Poem for the Bride	Poem for the Groom
Like bright,	Like flame,
like cool: the feel of	like star: the feel of you
you under me.	above me.
So young,	So strong,
so still: the loveliness	so swift: the river of you
of you under me.	above me.
Like bright,	Like flame,
like cool: let us be	like star: god in the dark
dark and happy.	and happy!

290

O thou whom Love has steeded,
Undered, harvested in joy—

Caressed divinely, O entered, owned,
Pierced by the stem divine—

Look now upon the divine boy
Breath lost, victor unbreathed, lost—

In the swoon of love: lone, most lone.
Hitched yet, embedded yet in love

Whiter than his sparks of love,
Whisper thou to his divine ear,

Love, O love, that I wert more thine!
That I could contain thee more . . .

Upon his breast heaving quietly,
Or upon his shoulder aglow yet

From strife: thy cheek lean tenderly,
Bestow a kiss from God.

291

Bridal Song

Love has learned to unclose me
                                    (this
the whiteness of the first sleep
between the lover and the loved).
                                    Reft
reft is the virgin dark: reft reft
is the music dark.
                    I am deeper now
than roses: whiter now than
rain washed in flowers:
                    O gentler
now than God.
For we are unclosed:
                    O we have rivered:
we have met: we are undeathed
by love!

292

Poem of the Man-God: The Lover

Only. And my whiteness
                    up the street of
into.

I did give. And was
not only.

                                    O nevermore
                    to be so only.

                                    293

                    The Sweet Song Sanora Sang
                    After the Setting of Sun

And it has been so long since my barren breasts
have shrunk without protest against the
breastbone of love.
                                Let my lover come bringing
limbs rich with long denials: I am the meadow
and the well, the hills of love and
the shade.

Come, let him darken me, let him seek
and desire, let him pierce and adore:
I am deeper than time, I enclose love,

                                            I enclose
love and her white divine dove . . .
Birds, mourn, O stars, mourn: mourn
for the night is not long: soon the lover must go

Must go my slim one, must go my dark one
(who has parts of dark, who has parts of steel:
he is steel and dark and divine.

Wine for my dove carries he
white divine wine
white divine wine for my white divine dove)

The talons of love fade with the sun,
blossoms of day arise: I am unwilling to leave night:
she has eternity in her eyes, music

nests deeper in her arms, the banners of love
unfold, glow, attain the eaglehood of star,
death becomes far

          And all this my heart
knows, all this my heart forever shall sing,
for my body has known love, my arms, my breasts
burst with the splendour of love!

294

And did you. Of her mouth
drink love?
          Which is to say.
O my young son. Was it
love? Were you
strong?
          Did she
lie soft? Was her hair
dark?
          Were the rivers
of you. Unafraid?
                    If this
be so. O my young son.
Adore. Adore.
                    Which is to say.
Return. Return.
Flower her feet
and hair.
          O never
let go. You did.
Drink love.

295

Address

And this plant
let be it of silver: or the goldth of green:
and the fruit: crimson: and deep silk:
as the pomegranate: as the tulip:
so that lovers adoring it
may learn the mystery of fire:
and the fairness of desire:
and they be victorious of love.
And under its silvern branches
let them taste of the deep fruit:
O the beautiful fruit: the godded fruit:
so that they be godded: as they were dreamt
by God. Let them lie
amorous and young: O prodigals of touch:
lover over young lover enparadised:
rivering: victorious of love.
And this was love:
is: and this will be love: as it was dreamt
by God. As it was dreamt by God.

296

Pretend we do not love
the heart not to bear:
Pretend
our lives were apart, untouching
our lips proud and unmet
our
bodies lone, young and inviolate:
O then there were not music,
there
were not God. There were not
eternity, there were not life!

297

Song Unworthy of Her

The woman enwombed with my son:
she is the flesh I have loved.
        Into her flesh I have writ
the signature of love. Cathedralled in her
sings the dawn of a son:
        She is the young mountain
of the sunrise: she is the dove fair-eagled
with love: she is the steel of tenderness
        between the lover and the loved.
I cannot write of her enough.
I cannot sing of her enough.

298

This thing so beautiful and high,
Imperial against an imperial sky,
Proud-browed and desolate,
Firm-chinned and immaculate,

This one brave and incorruptible,
Proud flame and imperishable,
Towards whom all the stars gaze
To learn her incandescent grace,

This lovely one is no ghost,
Nor soul homeless or lost,—
No, this one excels only Christ
By whom only she is best apprized.

—She is not War, nor Death, nor Peace,
But Love, footed upon a precipice.

299

Invitation to Doom

"Let me lead thee to thy doom,"
Quoth Love unto me,
                    "Let me take thee
By the hand, and kiss thee,
And break thee . . . Let me flame
                    into thy heart,
And dance there, and betray thee . . .
But all these, O my young one!
                    amidst rose-leaves
And rose-light, amidst fragrance
And damask, and the rose-curve
                    of my arms . . .
Wilt come, O my desired?
Wilt take the offer of my hand?"

                    Forthwith
I took the offer of her hand: I took—
The doom divine, by her hand divine.

300

Speech Against Love

But I have speech to say against love
But I have mouth to move against love
Music can not speak my speech
Music of love is glad

But I have music to speak against love
But I have speech to speak against love
Yet speech can not speak my speech
Speech of love is glad

And therefore it is not music
And therefore it is not speech
It is music against love
                    But no lover can sing it
It is speech against love
                    But no lover can say it

301

And of the golden road: the faméd road
And of the lonely road: the silver road

I have chosen the road of love: the silver road
I have chosen greatly: I have chosen whitely
        I have chosen the road to eternal sorrow

And if by the road of love: by the rosewoods
And if by the lake of love: by the rosewaters

I should fail ere I find the bowers of her feet
Let her hear of me: send her soft to me!
        Perish me not without the roses of her breasts!

302

One life is not enough for love—
I do so know it,
'Tis so much economy
For the Infinite!

Balance of eternity be so great—
There is no equal weigh,
But such parsimony
Be His diviner way.

Yet I would move His Hand so
Love could have ampler space,
If God would just move His Hand so,
O for Him, praise, praise!

303

From,peaches,are,polar,bears,made,
    From,bears,apples,from,pears,pearls,
As,from,love,truth,mercy,and,fire,
    And,from,fire,birds,peace,
And,the,cool,
    Twin,breasts,of,Eve.

From,bees,are,daisies,and,airplanes,made!
    From,tulips,lips,from,sunlight,sun,
As,from,man,truth,mercy,and,light,
    And,from,light,death,joy,
And,the,three,
    Heroic,hands,of,love.

304

A Song for Rosemarie

Why,lamps,are,lighted,
Why,eggs,are,gold,
I,do,not,know,no,
Sweet,heavens,no.

Pale,vermouth,ultraviolet,
And,tender,lambs,astray,
But,if,these,keep,love,beautiful,
Sweet,heavens,yes.

If,they,keep,love,beautiful,
Wych-tree,wych-bird,
Any,living,whyless,do,
In,that,living,kingdom,fire,

O,in,that,living,kingdom,love,
There's,never,living,no,
All,that's,living,is,yes,
Sweet,sweet,heavens,yes.

DUO-TECHNIQUE AND XOCERISMS

EDITOR'S NOTE ON DUO-TECHNIQUE: VILLA'S UNPUBLISHED VERSIFICATION METHOD

In the first three books Villa published in the United States he introduced three literary innovations: reversed consonance rhymes, the comma poem, and adaptations (known today as *found poems*). Villa's poetry innovation, Duo-Technique, is described in this centennial edition for the first time. With the benefit of Villa's handwritten notes, classroom lecture notes, and actual poems depicting duo-technique, I have reconstructed the poet's explanation of this new versification method he created three decades ago.

Villa once remarked to his workshop students that "duo-technique is a masterful breakthrough in modern-day versification and is as important to poetry as Cubism is to art. I must write something about it. Only you [John Cowen, Bob King, Mort Malkin, and Larry Francia] know about my invention of duo-technique."

On January 17, 1978, at a poetry workshop session given in his Greenwich Village apartment, Villa proceeded to give a brief explanation of his duo-technique versification method, prefacing his lecture by stating that he began work on his new technique during one of the previous semesters after failing to successfully rewrite an adaptation assignment. Villa's explanation of duo-technique is stated succinctly below:

> In all good verse, a tension like an inner nerve is pulling the lines technically together. Each tension goes from line to line, pulling a line downward toward its next line while, at the same time, pulling that line toward the preceding line. In traditional verse, the

overall technical tension is vertical or up and down. Also, there's a tension affected by pivot words at the end of each line. As I tried to reversify the poem to improve the tension using the normal way to versify up and down, vertically, it didn't sound right to me. The lines ran too fast with the normal technique. With the vertical technique alone, I could not modulate the line to satisfy my ear. To create the proper torque and tension, I moved out further to the right by creating an aisle or partition to create a horizontal tension. The horizontal tension is never there, except linguistically. Now by employing duo-technique, the poet can have two ways of creating the torque to modulate the sound and music of the poem: vertically and horizontally. The use of both techniques or duo-technique is a successful exploration of the medium, resulting in making spark-leaps across the gap between left and right sides.

An example of this vertical and horizontal movement is illustrated in a brief inscription, in the form of a little poem,* Villa wrote for a longtime student, Robert L. King, which employs duo-technique:

Breve Ars Humana

Let a man
   contain   an angel!

Yet let him
   not be   fully angel—

Though he
   Contain!   a Full Angel.

In a note, Villa lists five essential criteria for achieving this technique:

---

* This poem is a duo-technique adaptation of Aphorism 104.

Duo-Technique

1. A line of verse cut into 2 strips of language set apart as a single line
2. but, meant to be joined—
3. are left unjoined . . . thus, creating an aisle, a vertical partition of the poem—
4. yet, each partitioned line joins kinetically, invisibly—
5. through a valence of tensions that pull towards each other making spark-leaps across the gap between—left and right sides—like a poetic pas de deux.

The year 1976 marks the first recorded example of Villa's conscious use of duo-technique. This new method appears below in the form of an adaptation based on four lines from W. S. Merwin's twenty-one-line poem "Late Snow," which appeared on page 37 of the April 12, 1976, edition of *The New Yorker*. However, I also retrieved an earlier poem written by Villa that was apparently an unconscious attempt at using duo-technique, published in Manila in 1941 in *Poems by Doveglion*. This poem also follows, with its prescient title "Poem Designed by a Bird."

The unpublished adaptations that follow are based on snippets of prose and/or poems that Villa found pleasing to his ear or senses, but which were not satisfying enough to him as crafted. It should also be noted that the adaptations that follow were not intended for publication but were merely used by Villa as models to illustrate the craft and value of the duo-technique method to a small group of workshop students. These adaptations, however, are important vehicles because they illustrate how this versification method can enhance the medium and can be used deliberately in the future by poets who practice their craft, as others before them used sprung rhythm, slant rhyme, and the like, to enhance their poem's meter, rhythm, rhyme, or prosody.

JEC

DUO-TECHNIQUE POEMS
AND ADAPTATIONS

Poem Designed by a Bird

And so then
if a little
blue bird
came trip
ping love

        let music
        run to it
        let music
        say it heard
        let music

bloom in
flame: O
I am with
out shame
for love:

        I would be
        death if
        love would
        love me
        I would be

hate if
love would
take me: O
I would be
anything

```
                    for love:
                    because a
                    little blue
                    bird thought
                    love: yes
```

From *Poems by Doveglion* (The Philippine Writers' League).

Late Snow

```
            once
        we  wake
    ) and  it  has
            snowed        :        everywhere


            from
        the  railing
    you  wave  your
            arms          :        to the pines!


            )they're
        holding
    white  sky
            above         :        white ground


            )their
        own  feet
    still  asleep!
            in the        :        dark forest
```

Adapted from W. S. Merwin's "Late Snow," published in *The New Yorker*.

Finishing The Poem

More
brightly
with each word

the
daylight
shines!—

Such
radiance!
— creative —

ter-
minal.
Day's flush

Of
pleasure!
knowing its poem

grain
by coral
grain: *done*.

Adapted from James Merrill's "Clearing the Title,"
published in *The New Yorker*.

The water	hollows the stone, the wind
disperses	the water, the stone
stops the	wind:

| (water | (wind | (stone |

The wind   sculpts the stone,
                  the stone
is a cup   of water,
                  the water
runs off   — is wind:

(*wind*   (*water*   (*stone*

One is the   other — and is
                  neither!
among th'r   empty names
                  they pass
and dis-   appear

(*water*   (*wind*   (*stone*

Adapted from Octavio Paz (translated from Spanish by
Mark Strand), published in *The New Yorker*.

To get
the short pencil
point to make

                        A daring
                   Bridge between
              pencil and paper!

              —a metaphorical
                   bridge that can
                        carry from

Mind *to*
Paper . . . the lines
of a daring REAL

                              BRIDGE,
                         which can cause
                        jaws to drop, or

                        words of a daring
                             new philosophy
                                 to cause

             Eyebrows
          to arch! yet make
        us face ourselves.

Adapted from prose, Henry Petroski's *The Pencil* (Knopf).

Writing Poetry

    From this pencil,

                                 a path of
                        black lead—
                                 a letter

    making its way—

                                 Till here
                        is a *word*!
                                 till there

        is a Homestead

                             to reach:
                        tomorrow?—no,
                             today!

Adapted from prose, Henry Petroski's *The Pencil* (Knopf).

One
red bud
of pain   starts to open
                     in the heart—

the
gathering
sweetness   and expense
                     of spirit!

cells
flowing
over . . .   : a life twisting
                     into shape!

to
Golden
Honey   -comb . . . Full
                     silence now,

and
Salt
. . .   blossoming
                     in the heart.

Adapted from Eamon Grennan's, "Night Figure," published in *The New Yorker.*

Footprints

Now left
        foot—
now right
        foot—   We're arm
                     in arm with

regret !
        We

march up
            and   down in
                                   the earth and

take our
            flesh
in our
            teeth   Yet the wind
                               blows away our—

Adapted from Charles Wright's "The Silent Generation,"
published in *The New Yorker*.

(FEET ! !

—cheer-
ful cowards !   ready
                                   to whisk us
                                            away

—when
death calls . . .

(Or—
WHY feet *Love*   to dance!
                                  —to stay in
                                        shape

—for
Final Getaway!

Adapted from David Kirby's prose critique of Stephen Dobyns's poem "Feet,"
published in the *New York Times Book Review*.

In
the silence
            you   don't know—
                      you
                      must go

    on!
I *can't*
   go   on—*I'll*
            go
       on . . . !

Adapted from Samuel Beckett's short play *The Unnameable.*

At the Deli
(Ten Years Later)

Over
some table
   here (no

         X to mark
         the spot !)

Your
eyes would
   meet mine

         . . . in one
         thrilling

  thought
—*Last*
   night—(&

         nothing need
         be said!)

Adapted from Mary Jo Salter's "Inside the Midget,"
published in *The New Yorker.*

Thanks to NEA

PO   ETS!
         by the
         thousands

TRU   LY!
         America
        so recently

BAR   BAR
                 ous! only
                 yesterday

THE   WILD
                 West ! has
                 become — a

COUN   TRY
                 of no
                 body but

PE   OTS
                 roaming
                 the range!

Adapted from prose by Mark Harris: "Ah, The Poetry Reading,"
published in *The New York Times Book Review*.

With nothing to do   : but
                            : listen
                            : to

With nothing but signs   : between
                            : the
                            : lines

I study to die   : with ear
                            : to the
                            : sky

Adapted from Edward Newman Horn's "With nothing to do" from *The
Day Before the Day: Some of the Last Poems of Edward Newman Horn*
(Tideline Press)

Blue Storm

From His
        blue storm
    Christ
    calls out

to the
        believer: —
    "Sail up!
against

            "My Rock—
                and be
                shattered!
                —like

a dish."
        *(Would
    anyone?)*
Just how

            far! would
                God go
            in
            being God??

Adapted from Denis Johnson's novel *Resuscitation of a
Hanged Man* (Farrar, Straus and Giroux).

EDITOR'S NOTE ON VILLA'S UNPUBLISHED XOCERISMS

In José Garcia Villa's final years, he was writing with intensity, not poetry but about poetry—and intellect/intelligence, God, genius, love/sex/art, and life in all its facets. These aphorisms, or pensées, which Villa called his Xocerisms, are at once sharp, witty, insightful, and delightful. Like Montaigne, Pascal, and Merton, Villa writes his pensées, or Xocerisms, for truth about nature, art, and poetry to "say something new." And this Villa does with a charming uniqueness and stylistic form. Villa informs and delights the reader by his pithy expressions, through the torque and juxtaposition of words, thought, imagination, and wit—not quite poetry and, yet, not just prose. These Xocerisms are quite different from the aphorisms that appear in *Volume Two* and in *Selected Poems and New*. The aphorisms that first appeared in *Volume Two* were written using the poetic process; that is, they were inspired more from language rather than from thought. In other words, Villa's previous aphorisms read as poems do, not as prose. The newer aphorisms that Villa calls his Xocerisms are a unique form of expression, yet, still thought-provoking, wise, and akin to his poetry. David Daiches once praised Villa for his ability to look his subject in the eye, possessing the skill to, "Throw words unerringly at the center of the target." Marianne Moore agreed, commenting that "Final wisdom [is] encountered in poem after poem." Now, there is final wisdom encountered in Xocerism after Xocerism.

After Villa abandoned poetry, following the publication of *Selected Poems and New* (1958), he began expanding upon his major critical work, *The Theory of Poetry*, which remains unpublished. Villa contends, "My work is very structured. It is completely organized into a system. That is why I have been biding my time in releasing it. For more than three decades now, I have been at work on this series of related books: on language and the poetic process." By the sixties, he started writing addendum notes or aphorisms at a feverish pace; these poignant notes were extensions of his views on the poetic process, which he remained obsessed about for his entire life, and to which his every passing moment was devoted. His literary archives now contain nearly ten thousand of these notes, which mostly expand on his views of the poetic process but also touch on many of the subjects included in this selection of his Xocerisms.

From about 1990 to 1997, during the final seven years of his life, Villa began writing this new form of aphorism with greater determination and fervor, and which he deemed to be superior to the rest of his previous ones. He realized that these new aphorisms were much more focused and stylistic than any of his previous work, and to preserve these entries for future publication Villa began recording them in notebooks—rather than on loose paper scraps or the back of check deposit slips, as was his custom. It was at about this time, Villa stopped using the word *aphorisms* and began using his newly coined term, *Xocerisms*, when writing or speaking about this new phase of his work. Villa once explained that the term is a combination of his name, José, as it was written in Russian (Xoce) by his poet friend Yevgeny Yevtushenko, and the literary term *aphorism*.

Once when Villa's aphorisms were compared to Pascal's Pensées, he was quick to retort: "Don't compare Pascal's *Pensées* to mine—which I now call Xocerisms—pithy, inventive, philosophical insights told with a dash of Tabasco. His are flat, boring, simple-minded, and waddle like ducks in mud compared to mine." Villa was proud of his Xocerisms and believed that they might prove to be as important as his poetry one day. He believed that the aphorism is a very high artistic endeavor and even referred to writing them as a kind of graduation: "I have graduated for the third time in literature. First, I wrote short stories. Then I graduated by writing poems. Again I have graduated, and this time I am writing aphorisms—a higher art form than poetry." In his typical style, Villa once boasted, "My Xocerisms probe the ethic, philosophic force behind all essential living. And I do this in just one, two or three sentences at most." In one of his notebooks, Villa also created a visual tool that illustrates his view of the important stature of the aphorism, with the heading, "The Evolution of Good Writing" as shown below:

THE EVOLUTION OF GOOD WRITING

EXPANSIVENESS————ECONOMY————ESSENCE
(Novel, Story, Essay)   (Poetry)   (Aphorism)

Villa's notion of the poetic process evolved from his belief that lyrical poetry is the highest form of writing that is economical as well as musical. To illustrate this point, one of his most anthologized poems begins: "First, a poem must be magical, / Then musical as a sea-gull. / It must be a brightness moving. / And hold secret a bird's flowering. / It must be slender as a bell, / And it must hold fire as well . . ." Villa could just as well have inserted the term *aphorism* for "poem." He always championed the cause of economy of language, and his concise Xocerisms invoke a lyricism that employs a higher pitch of language or lilt and that creates a tonality quite different from most prose writing. This musicality and rhythm create his unique poetic-aphoristic style, if not a new genre: Villa's.

The Xocerisms that follow represent just a sampling from the hundreds of poetic aphorisms handwritten in his many notebooks. Another longtime student of Villa's, Mort Malkin, and I worked collaboratively for more than one year, selecting more than 150 Xocerisms, which we later categorized under the following headings: God, Nature, Beauty; Genius; Sex/Love; Art and Craft; Poets; Poetry; Peotry/Peots; Criticism and Critics; Intellect/Intelligence; Human Behavior; The Artist; Poetry and Prose Processes; and Linguistics.

A dozen notebooks or so remain to be mined, containing hundreds more of these poetic aphorisms. Therefore, a book of José Garcia Villa's collected Xocerisms is awaiting some interested publisher.

JEC

XOCERISMS

God, Nature, Beauty

1

God has no hormones, having delegated them to poets.

2

To reinvent God is unnecessary; all
He needs today is a Designer Name.

3

God is without scientific proof. Thank God!

4

No universal rainbows! All rainbows are local.

5

ANGELITY is the ideal *metaphysical* position for man.
Sainthood is too cruel, too costly; but angels can labor in
peace with men and God.

6

Poetry *without* ink? The poetry of the spirit is without ink.

7

God does not say Hello, He says, *"Ole!"*

8

God started with Space and Time, thus He created Light, then
Life, then Love. But only Love has difficulty in surviving.

9

Where are there square bubbles?

10

God's best friend: Not the Pope, not the priest, but the poet.

11

God is more difficult than mathematics—and yet just as easy.

12

You can't be an angel with only one wing.
(How about an angel with one wing and a *horn*?)

13

Knowing God as a name only leaves Him unknown;
only the Wrestler with God can truly *feel* Him.

14

In heaven are the sun and the night constellations—and the
black fires of heaven: the black holes that lasso in the dirt, to
cleanse the universe.

Genius

15

Genius—so capable of multiple aureoles, so capable of
turbulence.

16

The fine poet is an erotic Holy man.

17

It is the purpose of miracles to produce saints—but if the
miracle goes wayward . . . geniuses.

18

To read between the lines is Logic.
To read between the lines when there are no lines is Imagination.

19

When you stand in front of a wise man, however "clothed"
you are, you stand naked.

20

—Even accompanied, genius walks alone.

21

In the question: Unnoticed stands the truth erect.
In the answers: only devising logics.

22

GENIUS—The Inverted Man, standing on his head.

23

Shouldn't "immortals" be buried (fittingly) in space?

24

Genius is a mind of garlic-and-roses.

Sex/Love

25

Love is a giant prison without walls, and without guards, yet
there's no technology for escape.

26

Love is more vehement than God!

27

The love which begins with a tickle, or a smile, or a ling! ling!
—it does not matter which! For Love *has* begun.

28

Ah, sex—that epic of the night.

29

Love has no innovations—only sex has innovations.

30

Love may leave stains, yet with them also, leave flowers.

32

The word *menopause* is misnamed; it should be *femopause*.

33

I believe in the heart—in fact, I believe in every available organ.

34

Even in Rome, not every Roman does as Romans do.
Even in France, not every kiss is a French Kiss.

Art and Craft

35

Form is to Substance what a wet T-Shirt is to a fine body.

36

More important than *pregnancy* of line is *felicity* of line.

37

To be emancipated in art is to bind yourself to craft.

38

In art, you can't push if nothing is pushing back.

39

To find the language that *cuts*, may hurt—*yet heals*,
gives joy, gives light.

40

A matter of physics—Length and Tension—How does the
performer make it sing above the laws of sound?

41

Great art is never born at room temperature.

42

Art is a miraculous flirtation with *Nothing!*
Aiming for nothing, and landing on the Sun.

43

CRAFT is not only the structure of art but also its safety net.

44

Art is the How, not the What, of the work.

45

The absolute, straight line between two points is,
however, not the line of wit. Wit must *swerve* to whip.

46

There are imperfections so charming that they are perfect.

47

Art is not difficult because it wishes to be difficult but
because it wishes to be art.

48

A Silence that Answers a Silence that Questions.

49

A poem is language built to the structure of a flower.

(49)

A poem

                is

language
built

to the

              struc-

ture of a
flower.

Poets

50

The poet tangos with the cosmos, but why not?

51

True poets spring from DNA stardust of poetry,
not from poetry workshops.

52

Be of good Fear that in your poetry you are involuntarily
Naked!

53

A poet's poem should be like a fireman's fire—a risky danger,
a grand challenge, a heroic triumph.

54

Since he is introverted even in his extroverted language,
every good poet must be tethered to the sky.

55

Alas, there is no way, easy or hard, out of poetry.
It is his cage of gold.

56

If you write your poems at night, be sure that you can respect
them in the morning.

57

Language has secrets that only good poets can reveal.

58

Poets are not hungry; they hunger.

59

A poet, if he's a real poet, will be at the mercy of the poem.

Poetry

60

The difference between good poetry and great poetry
lies in the quality called wisdom.

61

Language, Music, Craft, & Sense (or Mystery)
:the *Quatrefoil & Quaternion* of poetry.

62

The poem's *First Line:* The coiled *cobra.*

63

A First Line that does not *wink* at the reader is
a dead, dead Line.

64

A poem is not a thought, but a grace.

65

Poetry is an angel with a gun in its hand.
Approach and you live. Depart and you die.

66

POETRY—The joy of language amidst the pain of existence.

67

Even prose can be poetic.
Only poetry can be *poetric*.

68

You can't *Think it* in prose and then *Write it* in poetry.

69

Poetry without *pizzazz* is like a cocktail party with no drinks.

70

Does the Poet become the Poem? Or the Poem become the Poet?

Peotry/Peots

71

PEOTRY and PEOTS are my coined words for *bad poetry* and *bad poets*.

72

Poems worth their weight in lead.

73

Most teachers of poetry, not only do not know their *onions*—they have *no* onions.

74

Ah, a Greek chorus unto himself: a ***cockalorum***.

75

They who, with all good will, use language
as an instrument of torture.

76

Poems there are that cannot survive the
cemeteries of their first lines.

77

Though miscast poets may have a love
for language, it is unrequited.

78

Humid writing: everything drips!

79

A bad poem is like a Wagnerian potato chip.

80

Lines that go *Pffft*.

Criticism and Critics

81

The future of Bad Poetry? *Wonderful!*

82

Magazines are full of poemburgers—but they don't
mean a thing ' 'cause they don't got that swing.'

83

A book of 50 poems—49 poems too long!

84

I'm not Simpleton-friendly. Hooray!
But neither am I Ph.D.-friendly. Hurrah!

85

Free verse is verse without a driver's license.

86

What about the *Prevention of Poetry?*

87
Sometimes it's better not to know what you know
than to "know" what you don't know.

88
—Stuff that makes your eyelids gain weight.

89
Should have his **BRAIN LOBES ROTATED**.

90
Ah, his Peanut Eminence!

91
A good critic makes you Tick; the bad critic makes you
paralytic.

92
Bad poems, I'm sure, despise their authors!

93
Naïve, faux ambition responds to a spider's invitation.

94
The poetaster's disease is **MESSAGE**.

95
At last, there is *AT LAST!*

Intellect/Intelligence

96
Reason is merely connecting the dots but intelligence
is the creation of those dots.

97
The refinement of one's language is ultimately
the refinement of one's mind.

98

Monks do not bait themselves with fatuous mundane
dreams, but live in abstract, painful peace.

99

Hard decisions are in quiet made, but in turmoiling stillness.

100

Nor Time nor cosmetics can unwrinkle age, but age may
counter with unwrinkled wisdom.

101

Minds that do not tick well do not tickle.

102

The intellect—the specializing mind—is fraught with heavy
analyses. The intelligence—the generic and generous mind
does not specialize but peregrinates like a wise butterfly to
discover joys.

103

There are Questions that outlast answers.

104

Do not confuse **Bingo!** (chance) with **Eureka!** (intellectual
effort)

105

THINKING is Abstracting: shearing off the *superfice*: and the
resultant thought is abstract: a stalwart Nude.

106

ABSTRACTION is the shorthand for essence: it erases
temporal matter for the eternal: The Phoenix after the flames.

107

What do you *Know* that you Don't *Know*?
What don't you Know that you **Know**?

Human Behavior

108
H-O-M-O S-A-P . . . Stop Right There!

109
I shall always respect a human being *more* than a work of art.

110
Heart be simple, mind be complex.

111
A man—just a speck in the world! Should he not just sign his
name with a *dot*?

112
Only in the silence—perfect places in life—can you *not*
complain: the womb and the tomb.

113
Which came first—the Apple? or the Snake?

114
The longer one's life, the longer one's list of accountabilities.

115
To err is human,
To purr, feline.

116
Before you *adopt* yourself, ask for the *bad* references.

117
There are quality-of-life offenses, Not to be forgiven.

118

New Jews:
>   Survival through education.
Ancient Jews:
>   Educated by survival.

119

In front of your mirrors, Stand. Salute yourself with your
right arm: in front of you, your image salutes with its *left*
arm . . . This is the conundrum of mirrors! Wherefore, do
mirrors lie? Of course they do.

120

Man is born Siamese to his shadow, and sometimes he is
only the Shadow's shadow.

121

There are only two lasting bequests we can hope to give our
children. One is roots, the other, wings.

122

While in love trance, sign nothing.

The Artist

123

The Artist—that Alien from Inner Space, with an intuitive
metaphysical understanding of the power and passion of
love—a golden intelligence of the spirit—the courage to call
out, to speak out. ***Enough*** and ***Not*** enough—together in one
clear voice.

124

The artist first learns art from God, who wakens him. Then God
assails and flails him with tutors, the master artists.

125

The artist problematizes, difficultizes his art: sets up hurdles, challenges, Blockages: he celebrates obstacles.

126

Does one buy flowers without a stem? Yet an Artist would pick up and admire a stemless one or even a broken blossom. Or an interesting twig, or even a bit of brilliant, broken glass.

127

The centered self—the Ego. It takes an artist to go Off-Center.

128

"I recognize your voice." One should be able to say that to a good singer—as to a good painter, a good poet, a good sculptor.

129

Art openings—making art the sanctuary of the uncivilized.

130

A blank page is perfect utopia. If you can write on it and still leave the page utopian, then you are a great writer.

131

The moving, exploring camera of the imagination discovers gems at unexpected intersections of life and mind.

132

An artist has nothing to say until his work utters it.

Poetry and Prose Processes

133

Switching from prose to poetry or vice versa: is like undergoing a SEX CHANGE.

134

The meaning of a poem is danced and sung by its language—
but the language is a *masked dancer*.

135

The Poetic Process operates without a compass yet
miraculously finds its North.

136

The prose writer makes things known *in* words; the poet
makes things known *as* words.

137

The novel is the longest distance between two points.
The short story is the shortest.
The poem is the congruence of the two points.

138

Prose, the good apple.
Poetry, the superb anti-apple.

139

The lyric factor—the chlorophyll of poetry.

140

It is the business of lovers to make love, and it is the
business of poets to create poetry: Two noble businesses—
without the business of business.

141

Prose is flat-chested, but poetry is curvaceous and luscious.

142

Poetry is antimatter and antigravity.
Otherwise it could not soar.

Linguistics

143
WIT is a game/play between the alphabet and the mind.

144
When should a fling be flung? Dang if I know!

145
L—most beautiful of letters; and 7—most beautiful of numbers—and Each, the capsized image of the other.

146
It is language that gives *form* to thought.

147
Beware of *indigent language.* But beware also of language with a breast implant. And also the language of *flatness*!

148
E. E. Cummings jazzed up language. Gertrude Stein boogie-woogied language. They made language with a *joie de vivre.*

149
A TYGER is a more ferocious image than Tiger.

150
CLICHES: The common hussies of language—the **bimbos.**

151
Poetry is a treasure hunt *for* language *by* language.

152
Move from OW to WOW! –from malady to melody.

153
Twist a zero at its middle—get 8.
Add a tail to zero's right side—get 9.

154
JUNQUE = junk made elegant.

Printed in the United States
by Baker & Taylor Publisher Services